LITERARY MANIA!

Treat yourself to a trivia test that will tickle your literary fancy. It's all here—from William Shakespeare to Sidney Sheldon, from Franz Kafka to Judith Krantz! You don't have to live in a library to be a literary lion! Sharpen your skills with these sample stumpers:

— What was the name of David Copperfield's optimistic land-lord?
— Who was the creator of "Green Eggs and Ham"?
— Name the inveterate enemy of Sherlock Holmes.
— What is the subtitle of Lewis Carroll's "Through the Look-ing Glass"?
— Who was Tom Sawyer's sweetheart?
— Name the country of giants twelve times the size of man in "Gulliver's Travels."
— What was Joseph Conrad's native language?
— What was the sequel to "Gentlemen Prefer Blondes"?
— Daniel Defoe's "Robinson Crusoe" was based on what real person's adventures?
— Where is the play "Our Town" set?

For the answers to these and more than 990 other fascinat-ing questions, keep on reading and surrender yourself to TRIVIA MANIA!

TRIVIA MANIA
by Xavier Einstein

TRIVIA MANIA has arrived! With enough questions to answer every trivia buff's dreams, TRIVIA MANIA covers it all—from the delightfully obscure to the <u>seemingly obvious</u>. Tickle your fancy, and test your memory!

LITERATURE

TRIVIA Mania

XAVIER EINSTEIN

ZEBRA BOOKS
KENSINGTON PUBLISHING CORP.

ZEBRA BOOKS

are published by

Kensington Publishing Corp.
475 Park Avenue South
New York, N.Y. 10016

Third printing: August 1984

Printed in the United States of America

TRIVIA MANIA: *Literature*

1) The part of Westminster Abbey that contains tombs of and monuments to many writers?

2) Hunt, Millais, Rossetti and Morris belonged to what brotherhood?

3) Whose love song contains these lines?
   In the room the women come and go
   Talking of Michelangelo.

4) Five by Graham Greene:
   "Brighton _____ "
   "The _____ of the Matter"
   "Our _____ in Havana"
   "The _____ American"
   "Travels with My _____ "

5) Joseph Conrad collaborated with whom on the novels "The Inheritors" and "Romance"?

6) From which Shakespeare play is this line taken:
   Dost thou think, because thou art virtuous, there shall be no more cakes and ale?

7) Some of Kafka's heroes are known by what initial?

. . . *Answers*

1. Poets' Corner

2. Pre-Raphaelite Brotherhood

3. "The Love Song of J. Alfred Prufrock" by T.S. Eliot

4. "Brighton Rock"
   "The Heart of the Matter"
   "Our Man in Havana"
   "The Quiet American"
   "Travels With My Aunt"

5. Ford Madox Ford

6. (Sir Toby Belch in) "Twelfth-Night"

7. K

8) Jack London joined what famous gold rush?

9) What were the members of Shakespeare's company of actors known as before being installed as members of the royal household?

10) Argentinian weaver of short complex tales?

11) "When _____ Things Happen to _____ People."

12) Two by Judith Krantz: "Princess _____ " and " _____ Daughter."

13) Chaucer was an actual person. True or false?

14) "Lorna Doone, A Romance of _____ ."

15) To whom did Shakespeare dedicate the sonnets?

16) Andrew M. Greeley wrote "Love's Pagan Heart." True or false?

17) Lawrence Ferlinghetti's "A Coney Island of the _____ ."

18) Name of David Copperfield's optimistic landlord?

19) Simone de Beauvoir's philosophical escort?

20) Creator of "Green Eggs and Ham"?

21) Who wrote the play "Blithe Spirit," the autobiography "Present Indicative," and the novel "Pomp and Circumstance"?

22) Who wrote the Berlin Stories upon which "Cabaret" was based?

. . . *Answers*

8. Klondike

9. The Chamberlain's Men

10. Jorge Luis Borges

11. "When Bad Things Happen to Good People"

12. "Princess Daisy" and "Mistral's Daughter"

13. True, he was born in the 1340s

14. Exmoor

15. Mr. W. H.

16. False, it was written by Patricia Matthews

17. "A Coney Island of the Mind"

18. Mr. Micawber

19. Jean-Paul Sartre

20. Dr. Seuss

21. Noel Coward

22. Christopher Isherwood

23) Who thought he'd never see a poem lovely as a tree?

24) He lived in a cottage in the Bronx.

25) Running writer?

26) "The Preppy Cat" — real book or just a notion?

27) Title of a series on Appalachian life styles?

28) Name the three Sitwells, a sister and two brothers.

29) French author Céline's real last name?

30) Robert Ludlum's foray into humor?

31) Leading Spanish poet executed in the Spanish Civil War?

32) Where did Victor Hugo spend his exile?

33) Author of "The Cruel Sea"?

34) He wrote "Room at the Top."

35) "Cruel _____ " by Steve Martin.

36) Author of "Memoirs of a Fox-Hunting Man"?

37) E.L. Doctorow's Western?

38) Gael Greene's "Blue Skies, No _____ ."

39) G. Gordon Liddy tells all.

40) Author of "Steppenwolf" and "Magister Ludi"?

41) George Eliot was her pen name.

. . . Answers

23. Joyce Kilmer

24. Edgar Allan Poe

25. Jim Fixx

26. Real book, publishing in 1982

27. Foxfire

28. Edith, Osbert and Sacheverell

29. Destouches

30. "The Road to Gandolfo"

31. Federico Garcia Lorca

32. The Channel Islands

33. Nicholas Monsarrat

34. John Braine

35. "Cruel Shoes"

36. Siegfried Sassoon

37. "Welcome to Hard Times"

38. "Blue Skies, No Candy"

39. "Will" by G. Gordon Liddy

40. Hermann Hesse

41. Mary Ann or Marian Evans

42) Louisa _____ Alcott wrote " _____ Women."

43) Nationality and current occupation of the heroine and hero in Hemingway's "A Farewell to Arms"?

44) She wrote "A Taste of Honey" when she was 18.

45) " _____ _____ Road Atlas," annual bestseller.

46) Author of "Scaramouche" and "Captain Blood"?

47) Which Latin poet was Dante's guide through the Inferno?

48) What is the protagonist's name in Dostoevski's "The Idiot"?

49) Shakespeare's early patron?

50) Date of Arthur C. Clarke's "Odyssey Two"?

51) First name of D.H. Lawrence's wife?

52) " _____ _____'s Workout Book."

53) "Where are the snows of yesteryear?" is what French vagabond poet's best known line?

54) Author of "Wampeters, Foma and Granfaloons"?

55) Feminist and author Gloria _____ .

56) Creator of the Lemon Drop Kid and Harry the Horse?

57) From which Shakespeare play is this line taken:
A thousand flatterers sit within thy crown,
Whose compass is no bigger than thy head . . .

. . . Answers

42. Louisa May Alcott wrote "Little Women"

43. She was an English nurse, he was an American lieutenant in the Italian ambulance service

44. Shelagh Delaney

45. "Rand McNally Road Atlas"

46. Rafael Sabatini

47. Virgil

48. Prince Myshkin

49. Henry Wriothesley, Earl of Southampton

50. 2010

51. Frieda

52. "Jane Fonda's Workout Book"

53. François Villon

54. Kurt Vonnegut

55. Steinem

56. Damon Runyon

57. (John of Gaunt in) "King Richard II"

58) In what surroundings was Dickens' "Little Dorrit" born?

59) Creator of "archy and mehitabel"?

60) Petrarch's ideal woman was named?

61) Sappho's island?

62) Author of "The Good Earth"?

63) "The Autobiography of Alice B. Toklas" was not written by her but by?

64) Boston cookbook author and TV personality?

65) John Ehrlichman's book was retitled "Washington Behind Closed Doors" for the TV tie-in—its original title?

66) What were the members of Shakespeare's company of actors known as after becoming members of the royal household?

67) Author of "Native Son"?

68) From which Shakespeare play is this line taken:
The eye of man hath not heard, the ear of man hath not seen, man's hand is not able to taste, his tongue to conceive, nor his heart to report, what my dream was.

69) Author of "My Mother/My/Self"?

70) Name of the boat's captain in "Jaws"?

71) Pirate and poet?

72) Sylvester Stallone is credited as author of the book "Rocky." True or false?

. . . *Answers*

58. Prison

59. Don Marquis

60. Laura

61. Lesbos

62. Pearl S. Buck

63. Gertrude Stein

64. Julia Child

65. "The Company"

66. The King's Men

67. Richard Wright

68. (Bottom in) "A Midsummer-Night's Dream"

69. Nancy Friday

70. Quint

71. Sir Walter Raleigh

72. False, it was written by Julia Sorel

73) Life of the Doors' Jim Morrison?

74) Playwright who married Marilyn Monroe?

75) What 19th century Russian medical doctor's short stories and plays are popular today in translation?

76) The captain's name in "Mutiny on the Bounty"?

77) Syndicated columnist on everyday problems who wrote an encyclopedia?

78) From which Shakespeare play is this line taken:
    Good night, good night! parting is such sweet sorrow
    That I shall say good night till it be morrow.

79) Author of "Gentlemen Prefer Blondes"?

80) Most famous of the medieval morality plays?

81) Scarlett's twin admirers in "Gone With the Wind"?

82) Did James Joyce win the Nobel Prize for Literature?

83) The Artful Dodger, Nancy, Bill Sikes, Charley Bates and Fagin star in which Dickens story?

84) Name of heroine in "Scruples"?

85) Dean Swift's name for his beloved Esther Johnson?

86) Correct or incorrect?
    Irving Wallace: The Origin
    Irving Stone: The Second Lady

87) Sylvia Plath's poet husband?

. . . Answers

73. "No One Gets Out of Here Alive"

74. Arthur Miller

75. Anton Chekhov

76. William Bligh

77. Ann Landers

78. (Juliet in) "Romeo and Juliet"

79. Anita Loos

80. "Everyman"

81. Stuart and Brent Tarleton

82. No

83. "Oliver Twist"

84. Billy Ikehorn

85. Stella

86. Incorrect, other way around

87. Ted Hughes

88) Pen name of Hector Hugh Munro?

89) A radio play for voices set in a Welsh village?

90) From which Shakespeare play is this line taken:
Death lies on her like an untimely frost
Upon the sweetet flower of all the field.

91) He wrote "The Horse's Mouth," basis of the Alec Guinness film.

92) Author of "A Town Like Alice," "The Far Country" and "On the Beach"?

93) Le Carré's George?

94) Temple Drake's life is covered in which two of Faulkner's books?

95) Author of "The Devil's Dictionary"?

96) He is popularly associated with Russia, butterflies and an American nymphet.

97) What's the family name in Eugene O'Neill's "Long Day's Journey into Night"?

98) From whch Shakespeare play is this line taken:
But when I tell him he hates flatterers,
He says he does, being then most flattered.

99) Joyce Jillson's answer to "Real Men Don't Eat Quiche"?

100) From which Shakespeare play is this line taken:
O! what a world of vile ill-favour'd faults
Looks handsome in three hundred pounds a year.

. . . Answers

88. Saki

89. "Under Milk Wood"

90. (Capulet in) "Romeo and Juliet"

91. Joyce Cary

92. Nevil Shute

93. Smiley

94. "Sanctuary" and "Requiem for a Nun"

95. Ambrose Bierce

96. Vladimir Nabokov

97. Tyrone

98. (Decius in) "Julius Caesar"

99. "Real Women Don't Pump Gas"

100. (Anne Page in) "The Merry Wives of Windsor"

101) What major Victorian novelist spent as much time working for the post office as he did writing?

102) A.A. Fair is a pen name of what well known detective writer?

103) Bernard Pomerance's play about the human spirit in a circus freak?

104) "Love in a Cold Climate" and "Noblesse Oblige" are by?

105) Setting of "Shogun"?

106) John Updike's literary assay into Africa?

107) Springtime bestselling do-it-yourself guides?

108) Which Athenian philosopher wrote nothing and is known to us mainly through the writings of one of his pupils?

109) In what city is there a streetcar named Desire?

110) Creator of Hercule Poirot?

111) "Chuck and _____ Have a Baby."

112) Female author of controversial young-adult bestsellers who turned her hand to adult bestsellers?

113) Reknowned critic of Henry James, James Joyce and Willa Cather?

114) She was less well known by the pen name Mary Westmacott.

115) How many lines in a sonnet?

. . . *Answers*

101. Anthony Trollope

102. Erle Stanley Gardner

103. "The Elephant Man"

104. Nancy Mitford

105. Japan

106. "The Coup"

107. Income tax guides

108. Socrates, through the writings of Plato

109. New Orleans

110. Agatha Christie

111. Di

112. Judy Blume

113. Leon Edel

114. Agatha Christie

115. 14

116) From which Shakespeare play is this line taken:
   I understand a fury in your words,
   But not the words.

117) Who wrote "Song of Myself"?

118) "Living, Loving and Learning" by Leo who?

119) William Dean Howells sued Mark Twain for libel. True or false?

120) From which Shakespeare play is this line taken:
   Why, then the world's mine oyster,
   Which I with sword will open.

121) Inspector Maigret's "precinct house"?

122) "Here lies one whose name was writ in water." Who?

123) Bryher's first name?

124) In "Much Ado About Nothing," Don Pedro's jealous and vindictive illegitimate brother?

125) "Some Came Running and "The Thin Red Line" were not as successful as his big 1951 novel. What was that and who was he?

126) From which Shakespeare play is this line taken:
   The gods sent not
   Corn for the rich men only.

127) Updike's " _____ Is Rich" and " _____ Is Back."

128) When someone came into the room, Jane Austen would quickly hide her manuscript page under a blotter. True or false?

. . . *Answers*

116. (Desdemona in) "Othello"

117. Walt Whitman

118. Buscaglia

119. False, they were always on good terms

120. (Pistol in) "The Merry Wives of Windsor"

121. Quai des Orfèvres

122. John Keats

123. Winifred

124. Don John

125. "From Here to Eternity" by James Jones

126. (Caius Marcius Coriolanus in) "Coriolanus"

127. "Rabbit Is Rich" and "Blech Is Back"

128. True

QUESTIONS

129) First names of Elizabethan dramatists Beaumont and Fletcher?

130) Two by Jeffrey Archer: "Kane _____ _____ " and "The _____ Daughter."

131) Creator of "Peter Pan"?

132) Henry Miller's "Tropic of Cancer" is set in what city?

133) South American terrorists kidnap a harmless, boozy Briton by mistake instead of the American ambassador. Title and author?

134) In Homer's Greek version he is called Odysseus, and in Virgil's Latin version he is called?

135) What did Poe's raven answer?

136) "Tom Brown's Schooldays" was set at what English public school?

137) "A Not-So-Still Life," autobiography by artist son of artist father Max. Son's name?

138) Donizetti's opera "Lucia di Lammermoor" is based on what novel by what author?

139) From which Shakespeare play is this line taken:
There is no more mercy in him than there is milk in a male tiger . . .

140) Author of "Blackboard Jungle"?

141) Dante's ideal woman was named?

142) Who was the first original poet in North America?

. . . Answers

129. Francis Beaumont, John Fletcher

130. "Kane and Abel" and "The Prodigal Daughter"

131. J.M. Barrie

132. Paris

133. "The Honorary Consul" by Graham Greene

134. Ulysses

135. "Nevermore"

136. Rugby

137. Jimmy Ernst

138. "Bride of Lammermoor" by Sir Walter Scott

139. (Menenius in) "Coriolanus"

140. Evan Hunter

141. Beatrice

142. Ann Bradstreet (1612?-1672), of Massachusetts Bay Colony

143) Steven Spielberg is credited as author of the book "Close Encounters of the Third Kind." True or false?

144) What French writer was refused a Christian burial in 1778, and in 1791 was interred with national honors in the Pantheon?

145) What did Bartleby the Scrivener reply to all entreaties?

146) From which Shakespeare play is this line taken:
Go to your bosom;
Knock there, and ask your heart what it doth know . . .

147) "Cry, the Beloved Country" by Alan Paton is about what country?

148) " _____ Weighs In," " _____ Takes the Cake," " _____ Tips the Scale."

149) What poem, by what American poet, has this first line?
I saw the best minds of my generation destroyed by madness, starving hysterical naked,

150) Finish the titles: "Morte _____ ," "The Romance of the _____ ," "Sir Gawaine and the _____ _____ ."

151) Italian playwright responsible for "Six Characters in Search of an Author"?

152) Oxford Movement churchman who wrote "Apologia Pro Vita Sua"?

153) Who wrote this line?
If winter comes, can spring be far behind?

154) Some who never heard of him know by heart his "The Shooting of Dan McGrew."

. . . Answers

143. True

144. Voltaire

145. "I should prefer not to."

146. (Isabella in) "Measure for Measure"

147. South Africa

148. Garfield

149. "Howl" by Allen Ginsberg

150. "Morte d'Arthur," "The Romance of the Rose," "Sir Gawaine and the Green Knight"

151. Luigi Pirandello

152. John Henry Newman

153. Percy Bysshe Shelley

154. Robert Service

QUESTIONS

155) Goethe's "Faust" was based on a real person by that name. True or false?

156) A Catholic priest who writes fiction about some very unholy churchmen?

157) Martin Cruz Smith in Moscow?

158) Can you name the Shakespeare play from this ultra short plot summary:
    A boat is washed ashore on an enchanted isle.

159) Two by Alan Sillitoe: " _____ Night and _____ Morning" and "The Loneliness of the _____ _____ _____ ."

160) Two plays by Synge: "Riders to the _____ " and "In the Shadow of the _____ ."

161) Two by John Irving: "The _____ According to _____ " and "The _____ New _____ ."

162) Where do the adventures of "The Swiss Family Robinson" take place?

163) Goldsmith's play in which the hero mistakes the home of his wife-to-be as an inn, and her father as an overfamiliar inn-keeper?

164) Rex Stout's overweight gourmet detective who rarely bothers to leave his house to solve a crime?

165) Where was Kurt Vonnegut's protagonist when the Allies firebombed Dresden?

166) Virgil and Horace conducted a blood feud. True or false?

. . . Answers

155. True, Georg Faust (1480?-?1538)

156. Andrew M. Greeley

157. "Gorky Park"

158. "The Tempest"

159. "Saturday Night and Sunday Morning" and "The Loneliness of the Long Distance Runner"

160. "Riders to the Sea" and "In the Shadow of the Glen"

161. "The World According to Garp" and "The Hotel New Hampshire"

162. On a desert island

163. "She Stoops to Conquer"

164. Nero Wolfe

165. Working in that city, as a German prisoner of war, in an underground meat locker of a slaughterhouse

166. False, they were friends

167) Author of "Cornhuskers," "Smoke and Steel" and "Abraham Lincoln?"

168) Who said "Thank God for books as an alternative to conversation"?
   a. W. H. Auden
   b. J. D. Salinger
   c. Gore Vidal

169) The pen name under which Colette's first husband published her early novels as his own?

170) Story of Valium addiction?

171) New England poet Robert Frost was born where?

172) The face in the portrait ages while its subject remains young and handsome. Book and author?

173) Polish polo-player

174) In Waugh's "Decline and Fall," who does the teacher hero fall in love with and with what result?

175) T. S. Eliot was born in what American city?

176) From which Shakespeare play is this line taken:
   For never any thing can be amiss,
   When simpleness and duty tender it.

177) "Nothing Down" and "Creating Wealth" tell you how to make money through what?

178) God's in his heaven,
   All's _____ with the _____ .

. . . Answers

167. Carl Sanburg

168. a

169. Willy

170. "I'm Dancing as Fast as I Can"

171. San Francisco

172. "The Picture of Dorian Gray" by Oscar Wilde

173. Jerzy Kosinski

174. He falls in love with the mother of one of his pupils, and is unjustly charged with helping her in the white slave trade

175. St. Louis, MO

176. (Theseus, Duke of Athens, in) "A Midsummer-Night's Dream"

177. Real estate

178. "All's right with the world," from Robert Browning

179) Two by Sidney Sheldon: "A _____ in the Mirror" and "The _____ _____ of Midnight."

180) Alice receives advice from _____ , which sits on a mushroom and quietly smokes a long hookah?

181) What were the first and middle names of Sinclair Lewis' "Babbitt"?

182) Author of "The Wonderful Wizard of Oz"?

183) From which Shakespeare play is this line taken:
    Alas! poor Yorick. I knew him, Horatio . . .

184) Two by Muriel Spark: "The _____ of Peckham Rye" and "The _____ of Miss Jean Brodie."

185) First names of the three Brontë sisters?

186) Creator of Peter Rabbit, Benjamin Bunny and Tom Kitten?

187) A Danish baroness who lived for more than 15 years on a coffee plantation in British East Africa

188) Author of "The Women's Room"?

189) Two by Anne Rice: " _____ with the Vampire" and " _____ to Heaven."

190) Title of Howard Fast's novel on the Roman gladiator who led an insurrection of slaves?

191) Three Dorset brothers, all well known writers?

192) From which Shakespeare play is this line taken:
    To be or not to be: that is the question . . .

. . . *Answers*

179. "A Stranger in the Mirror" and "The Other Side of Midnight"

180. A large blue caterpillar

181. George Folansbee Babbitt

182. L. Frank Baum

183. (Hamlet in) "Hamlet"

184. "The Ballad of Peckman Rye" and "The Prime of Miss Jean Brodie"

185. Charlotte, Emily, Anne

186. Beatrix Potter

187. Isak Dinesen, pen name of Baroness Karen Blixen

188. Marilyn French

189. "Interview with the Vampire" and "Cry to Heaven"

190. "Spartacus"

191. J.C., Llewelyn and T.F. Powys

192. (Hamlet in) "Hamlet"

193) Upon what does Sandra Boynton's "Consuming Passion" fall?

194) Name the Brontë dissipated brother.

195) After Mark Twain, who was the most popular writer in America at the turn of the century? Not an American.

196) From which Shakespeare play is this line taken:
There was speech in their dumbness, language in their every gesture. . .

197) How many years did the Greeks fight to recover Helen from Troy, and how much is covered in the "Iliad"?

198) Author of "The Deserted Village"?

199) Daddy of "Mafia Princess"?

200) Sir Arthur Conan Doyle's other profession?

201) How many people did King Arthur's Round Table seat, and how many of those places were always left vacant?

202) "Pigeons of the grass alas" is from whose libretto for what opera?

203) Theatre in Dublin where the plays of O'Casey and Yeats were first staged?

204) From which Shakespeare play is this line taken:
How weak a thing
The heart of woman is.

205) Stephen Dedalus is what author's alter ego?

. . . Answers

193. Chocolate

194. Patrick Branwell Brontë

195. Rudyard Kipling

196. (A gentleman in) "The Winter's Tale"

197. Ten years, in which only the final year is described in the "Iliad"

198. Oliver Goldsmith

199. Sam Giancana

200. Medical doctor

201. The Round Table seated 151, of which one place was always left vacant for the finder of the Holy Grail

202. Gertrude Stein's, for "Four Saints in Three Acts"

203. Abbey Theatre

204. (Portia in) "Julius Caesar"

205. James Joyce's

206) What is the name of the book that gave Machiavelli a Machiavellian reputation?

207) Samuel Beckett's play "Krapp's Last _____ ."

208) L.A. cop turned author?

209) Ed Koch tells us about the most unforgetable and forgetable characters he has met.

210) Author of "Middlemarch"?

211) Macavity the Mystery Cat, Gus the Theatre Cat, Bustopher Jones the Cat about Town and Skimbleshanks the Railway Cat are personalities in what book?

212) Correct or incorrect?
    Sir Walter Raleigh: History of the World
    Thomas More: Utopia

213) Who wrote the play "Mourning Becomes Electra"?

214) "The Silent Spring" (1962) made many conscious of dangers to the environment. Its author?

215) Writer and historian first on the New Deal and later on the Kennedys?

216) From which Shakespeare play is this line taken:
    Give me some music; music, moody food
    Of us that trade in love.

217) Bernard Malamud has written accounts of his conversations with a Mexican Indian medicine man. True or false?

218) Karl Marx's big blockbuster?

. . . Answers

206. "The Prince"

207. "Krapp's Last Tape"

208. Joseph Wambaugh

209. "Mayor"

210. George Eliot

211. "Old Possum's Book of Practical Cats" by T.S. Eliot

212. Correct

213. Eugene O'Neill

214. Rachel L. Carson

215. Arthur M. Schlesinger, Jr.

216. (Cleopatra in) "Antony and Cleopatra"

217. False

218. "Das Kapital" ("Capital")

219) In which Tennessee Williams play is one of the characters killed and devoured by a mob of starving children?

220) Name of manuscript collection of Old English poetry, c. 975 A.D., which contains "The Seafarer" and "The Wanderer"?

221) Title of Edward Albee's first produced play?

222) Russian poet who married Isadora Duncan?

223) How old was Huck Finn at the time of his adventures?

224) From which Shakespeare play is this line taken:
    The venom clamours of a jealous woman
    Poison more deadly than a mad dog's tooth.

225) Author of "Ship of Fools"?

226) Name of King Arthur's sword?

227) Strunk and White's manual of instruction?

228) Biographer of Ernest Hemingway and Sophia Loren?

229) First book of John Le Carré in which a woman is the most important character?

230) "187 Ways to Amuse a Bored Cat" by Howe and Ruth Stidger—real book or just a notion?

231) The author of the line "I was not waving but drowning" had a successful movie made about her life in a London suburb—her name?

232) Three by Louis L'Amour: "The Lonesome _____ ," "The Cherokee _____ " and "The Shadow _____ ."

. . . *Answers*

219. "Suddenly, Last Summer"

220. Exeter Book (Codex Exoniensis)

221. "Zoo Story"

222. Sergei Esenin

223. About 12

224. (The Abbess in) "The Comedy of Errors"

225. Katherine Anne Porter

226. Excalibur

227. "The Elements of Style"

228. A.E. Hotchner

229. "The Little Drummer Girl"

230. Real book, published in 1982

231. Stevie Smith

232. "The Lonesome Gods," "The Cherokee Trail," The Shadow Riders"

233) What gave O. Henry the time to write short stories instead of newspaper reporting?

234) " _____ _____ Best of Helpful Hints."

235) Shakespeare, Jonson, Raleigh, Beaumont and Fletcher were among the customers at what famous Cheapside tavern?

236) William Faulkner was awarded the Novel Prize for Literature. True or False?

237) "The Great Shark Hunt" was:
   a. a study of Detroit car executives
   b. a Greenpeace exposé
   c. the sequel to "Jaws"
   d. a survey of the 1960s

238) Creator of James Bond?

239) _____ Neruda, Chilean poet.

240) "Rolling Stone Visits Saturday Night Live" — real book or just a notion?

241) French author (1825–1915) of a ten-volume work on insect life?

242) From which Shakespeare play is this line taken:
   No visor does become black villainy
   So well as soft and tender flattery.

243) Where did Pegasus, the winged horse, come from?

244) Who wrote the words "Glory be to God for dappled things"?

. . . Answers

233. A three-year term for embezzlement in Texas

234. "Mary Ellen's Best of Helpful Hints"

235. Mermaid Tavern

236. True in 1949

237. d

238. Ian Fleming

239. Pablo

240. Real book, published in 1979

241. Jean Henri Fabre

242. (Gower in) "Pericles"

243. Pegasus sprang from the blood of Medusa when she was decapitated by Perseus

244. Gerard Manley Hopkins

245) Edwin O'Connor is supposed to have based this portrait of a big city political boss and his shenanigans on Boston's mayor James M. Curley. Its title?

246) "2001" author Arthur C. Clarke lives in what country?

247) From which Shakespeare play is this line taken:
What fool is not so wise
To lose an oath to win a paradise

248) Louis has an unlikely last name for a writer of Westerns.

249) What are the two cities in Dicken's "A Tale of Two Cities"?

250) The Romans Plautus, Terence and Seneca were:
a. playwrights
b. pastoral poets
c. military historians

251) Famous Scottish-born writer-naturalist who walked all over North America before the turn of the 20th century?

252) Author of "God Emperor of Dune"?

253) The "grasping old sinner" of Dickens' "A Christmas Carol"?

254) John Dos Passos, W. H. Auden, Jacques Barzun, Theodore Roethke and Lewis Mumford all received what fellowship?

255) Two by Robert Ludlum: "The _____ Covenant" and "The _____ Identity."

256) "The _____ _____ of Walter Mitty."

. . . *Answers*

245. "The Last Hurrah"

246. Sri Lanka (Ceylon)

247. (Longaville in) "Love's Labour's Lost"

248. L'Amour

249. London and Paris

250. a

251. John Muir

252. Frank Herbert

253. Ebenezer Scrooge

254. Guggenheim

255. "The Holcroft Covenant" and "The Bourne Identity"

256. "The Secret Life of Walter Mitty"

257) Three by William Golding:
"Pincher _____ "
"Lord of the _____ "
"Free _____ "

258) First names of the two Durrell brothers?

259) Donald Sutherland was in the movie set on an island and based on which book by Ken Follett?

260) Author of "The Winds of War" and "War and Remembrance"?

261) From which Shakespeare play is this line taken:
O mischief! thou art swift
To enter in the thoughts of desperate men

262) "Deep Throat" star turned author.

263) Correct or incorrect?
Livy: Germania
Tacitus: History of Rome

264) "Thin Thighs in _____ Days" — how many?

265) From which Shakespeare play is this line taken:
I have no other but a woman's reason:
I think him so because I think him so.

266) Two by Sidney Sheldon: " _____ of the Game" and
" _____ of Angels"?

267) Cicero and Julius Caesar were initially friends but later enemies. True or False?

. . . *Answers*

257. "Pincher Martin," "Lord of the Flies," "Free Fall"

258. Lawrence and Gerald

259. "The Eye of the Needle"

260. Herman Wouk

261. (Romeo in) "Romeo and Juliet"

262. Linda Lovelace

263. Incorrect, other way around

264. 30

265. (Lucetta in) "The Two Gentlemen of Verona"

266. "Master of the Game" and "Rage of Angels"

267. True

268) "The Decameron" was written by:
   a. Boccaccio
   b. Cellini
   c. Machiavelli
   d. Dante

269) "The Bronx Diet" — real book or just a notion?

270) Expert witness on love signs:
   a. Sylvia Porter
   b. Susan Brownmiller
   c. Linda Goodman
   d. Barbara Tuchman

271) The N.Y. Times Book Review described her autobiography as "a Brooklyn ghetto girl's progress to three homes, two Oscars, six mink coats and ninety-nine films." Whose?

272) Where were Chaucer's pilgrims going?

273) Stephen R. Donalson's chronicles?

274) "The Third World War" by General Sir John Hackett and other NATO generals, predicted that this conflict would start in:
   a. February 1984
   b. August 1985
   c. September 1991
   d. May 2003

275) Two My M. M. Kaye: "The Far _____ " and " _____ in Zanibar"?

276) "Free to Choose" was a tie-in to what Nobel economist's TV series?

277) Life at West Point according to Lucian K. Truscott IV?

. . . *Answers*

268. a

269. Real book, in answer to Westchester, published in 1979

270. c

271. Shelley Winters'

272. Canterbury

273. The Chronicles of Thomas Covenant

274. b

275. "The Far Pavilions" and "Death in Zanzibar"

276. Milton Friedman

277. "Dress Gray"

278) He wrote "Dracula," she wrote "Frankenstein."

279) From which Shakespeare play is this line taken:
     If all the year were playing holidays,
     To sport would be as tedious as to work . . .

280) Emerson, Longfellow, Whittier, Agassiz and Lowell were all members of what club?

281) From which Shakespeare play is this line taken:
     Press not a falling man too far; 'tis virtue:
     His faults lie open to the laws; let them,
     Not you, correct him.

282) One of the most successful plays of the 1890s was "The Second Mrs. Tanqueray," by what playwright?

283) Remember Erma Bombeck's "The Grass Is Always Greener _____ _____ _____ _____ "?

284) Title of each of the six volumes of Winston Churchill's "The Second World War"?

285) One by Ken Follett: "The _____ from St. Petersburg."

286) In Sinclair Lewis' "Main Street," what was the name of the typical American town?

287) T. S. Eliot released a live pigeon under his chair at a staid London restaurant. True or false?

288) Year "Gone with the Wind" was published and name of its author?

289) In Dana's "Two Years Before the Mast," what seafarers lived in an abandoned oven on the beach at San Diego?

. . . *Answers*

278. Bram Stoker, Mary Shelley

279. (Henry, Prince of Wales, in) "First part of King Henry IV"

280. The Saturday Club

281. (Lord Chamberlain in) "King Henry VIII"

282. Arthur Wing Pinero

283. "The Grass Is Always Greener Over the Septic Tank"

284. 1: "The Gathering Storm"; 2: "Their Finest Hour"; 3: "The Grand Alliance"; 4: "The Hinge of Fate"; 5: "Closing the Ring"; 6: "Triumph and Tragedy"

285. "The Man from St. Petersburg"

286. Gopher Prairie

287. True

288. 1936, Margaret Mitchell

289. Sandwich Islanders (Hawaiians)

290) Known as a composer and champion of serendipity, he is also the author of short ironic pieces.

291) From which Shakespeare play is this line taken:
Double, double toil and trouble:
Fire burn and cauldron bubble.

292) Two by Brian Moore: "The _____ _____ of Judith Hearne" and "The _____ of Ginger Coffey."

293) Where did Huck meet Jim?

294) Who wrote "Marathon Man," "Magic" and "Tinsel"?

295) Name of Russian writer sent to death camp for comparing Stalin's moustaches to cockroaches?

296) Correct or incorrect?
Irwin Shaw: Bread Upon the Waters
Thomas Harris: Red Dragon

297) Long train journeys are the nonfiction specialty of this novelist.

298) Known in Rome for his epigrams, he published his first book to celebrate the opening of the Coliseum. His name?

299) Real name and profession of Lewis Carroll, author of "Alice's Adventure's in Wonderland"?

300) Can you name the Shakespeare play from this ultra short plot summary:
The king's second son treacherously disposes of rebels while the first son carouses.

301) Author of "The Daring Young Man on the Flying Trapeze" and "The Time of Your Life"?

. . . Answers

290. John Cage

291. (The three witches in) "Macbeth"

292. "The Lonely Passion of Judith Hearne" and "The Luck of Ginger Coffey"

293. Jackson's Island

294. William Goldman

295. Osip Mandelstam

296. Correct

297. Paul Theroux

298. Martial

299. The Rev. Charles Lutwidge Dodgson was a mathematics lecturer at Christ Church, Oxford

300. "Part Two of Henry IV"

301. William Saroyan

302) Meryl Streep appeared in movies based on these books, one set in Lyme Regis, the other in Brooklyn.

303) From which Shakespeare play is this line taken:
   A horse! a horse! my kingdom for a horse!

304) What happened to Dostoevski's father?

305) Did George Bernard Shaw win the Nobel Prize for Literature?

306) What political office did Norman Mailer run for?

307) Correct or incorrect?
   Laurie McBain: Love Me Marietta
   Jennifer Wilde: Dark Before the Rising Sun

308) George Jean Nathan wrote about what?

309) What did Daniel Defoe call his account of the 1665 outbreak of bubonic plague in England?

310) Author of "Titus Groane" and "Gormenghast"?

311) From which Shakespeare play is the line taken:
   Who seeks, and will not take when once 'tis offer'd,
   Shall never find it more.

312) In Tennesee Williams' "The Rose Tattoo," where is the tattoo located?

313) Dr. Johnson's biographer?

314) Xaviera _____ had lots of love advice, which first appeared in "The Happy _____ ."

315) Author of "The Scarlet Pimpernel"?

... Answers

302. "The French Lieutenant's Woman" and "Sophie's Choice"

303. (King Richard in) "King Richard III"

304. He was murdered by his serfs in 1844

305. Yes, in 1925

306. He ran unsuccessfully for Mayor of New York City in 1969

307. Incorrect, other way around

308. The theatre

309. "A Journal of the Plague Year"

310. Mervyn Peake

311. (Menas in) "Antony and Cleopatra"

312. The truckdriver's chest

313. James Boswell

314. Xaviera Hollander in "The Happy Hooker"

315. Baroness Orczy

QUESTIONS

316) William Manchester referred to Gen. Douglas MacArthur as an American Caesar. True or false?

317) Author of "A Distant Mirror" and "The March of Folly"?
   a. Leon Uris
   b. James A. Michener
   c. Barbara W. Tuchman
   d. Alistair Cooke

318) The kind doctor takes a drug that transforms him into a demon, in what story by what author?

319) Edward Gibbon wrote "The Decline and Fall of the _____ Empire"?
   a. Russian
   b. Indian
   c. Roman
   d. British

320) Author of "Breakfast at Tiffany's"?
   a. Jaqueline Susanne
   b. Truman Capote
   c. Gore Vidal
   d. William F. Buckley

321) Author of "I, Claudius" and "Claudius the God," basis for the PBS television series?

322) Four by Saul Bellow:
   "Dangling _____ "
   "Seize the _____ "
   "Looking for _____ _____ "
   "Henderson the _____ _____ "

323) Sequel to "Gentlemen Prefer Blondes"?

. . . Answers

316. True

317. c

318. "The Strange Case of Dr. Jekyll and Mr. Hyde" by Robert Louis Stevenson

319. c

320. b

321. Robert Graves

322. "Dangling Man"
"Seize the Day"
"Looking for Mr. Green"
"Henderson the Rain King"

323. "But Gentlemen Marry Brunettes"

324) Correct or incorrect?
   Francis Bacon: The Book Named the Governor
   Thomas Elyot: Novum Organum

325) King Lear had three daughters, named?

326) From which Shakespeare play is this line taken:
   Neither a borrower nor a lender be:
   For loan oft loses both itself and friend . . .
   This above all: to thine own self be true . . .

327) Can you name the Shakespeare play from this ultra short plot summary:
   Urged on by his wife, a man murders his king in order to take his place.

328) Prince of Norway who claims the Danish throne after Hamlet's death?

329) Lysias, Isocrates, Aeshines and Demosthenes were all:
   a. playwrights
   b. philosophers
   c. orators
   d. historians

330) Julius Caesar is told to beware the Ides of March, which is what day on the modern calendar?

331) This lady shapes up those dogs in print and on the tube.

332) "The Expedition of Humphrey Clinker" was by:
   a. Henry Fielding
   b. Laurence Sterne
   c. Tobias Smollett

. . . Answers

324. Incorrect, the other way around

325. Cordelia, Goneril, Regan

326. (Polonius in) "Hamlet"

327. "Macbeth"

328. Fortinbras

329. c

330. March 15th

331. Barbara Woodhouse

332. c

333) French writer and philosopher of personal happiness and freedom who placed all five of his children in an orphan asylum?

334) How many syllables in a Japanese haiku?

335) As poet John Berryman leaped to his death in 1972 from a bridge into the Mississippi, what was his last gesture reputed to be?

336) From which Shakespeare play is this line taken:
     An honourable murderer, if you will;
     For nought did I in hate, but all in honour.

337) Creator of Lady Sneerwell and Lady Teazle in "The School for Scandal"?

338) Title of Morley Callaghan's recollections of Hemingway, Fitzgerald and the lost generation?

339) "The Simple Cobler of Aggawam in America" was a 1647 New England tract denouncing just about everyone. True or false?

340) Correct or incorrect?
     Rosalind: As You Like It
     Rosaline: Romeo and Juliet

341) Max and Friedrich are both Swiss playwrights who write in German.

342) What was Joseph Conrad's native language?

343) Ex-wife of New York City American-Chinese psychoanalyst who became top-selling writer.

Answers

333. Jean Jacques Rousseau

334. 17

335. As he fell, he waved casually to a passerby

336. (Othello in) "Othello"

337. Richard Brinsley Sheridan

338. "That Summer in Paris"

339. True

340. Correct

341. Max Frisch and Friedrich Dürrenmatt

342. Polish

343. Erica Jong

344) Can you name the Shakespeare play from this ultra short plot summary:

By guile, a woman conceives a child with the man she loves and steals a ring from his finger.

345) Edmund Spenser referred to her as "Gloriana," Sir Philip Sidney was a friend, William Shakespeare performed his plays for her. Who?

346) Author "Tropic of Cancer"?

347) Famed writer of Westerns Max Brand also wrote about a modern medical doctor named what?

348) Ernest Hemingway had an irrational fear of seagulls. True or false?

349) The creator of Inspector Maigret?

350) From which Shakespeare play is this line taken:

What's in a name? that which we call a rose
By any other name would smell as sweet . . .

351) American poet who died in a taxi on way from airport into New York City?

352) What happened to Shakespeare's son?

353) " _____ versus _____ " by Avery Corman was made into a movie with Dustin Hoffman.

354) Ichabod Crane was a character in what book by what writer?

355) Remember James Herriot's "All Things _____ and _____ "?

. . . Answers

344. "All's Well That Ends Well"

345. Elizabeth I

346. Henry Miller

347. Dr. Kildare

348. False

349. Georges Simenon

350. (Juliet in) "Romeo and Juliet"

351. Robert Lowell

352. He died in boyhood

353. "Kramer versus Kramer"

354. "The Legend of Sleepy Hollow" by Washington Irving

355. "All Things Wise and Wonderful"

356) Survivor of the West Coast sixties who likes whimsical titles, such as "A Confederate General from Big Sur"?

357) English writer who made much of the idea that science and the humanities have split into two cultures?

358) She was born in Virginia but used Nebraska as the setting for much of her best fiction.

359) Norman Cousins' account of his fight against illness?

360) From which Shakespeare play is this line taken:
Be not afraid of greatness: some are born great, some achieve greatness, and some have greatness thrust upon them.

361) Author of "National Velvet"?

362) Who wrote these lines?
Stone walls do not a prison make,
Nor iron bars a cage?

363) Correct or incorrect?
John Le Carré: Blood and Money
Thomas Thompson: The Honourable Schoolboy

364) "Specimen Days" is Walt Whitman's diary account of what?

365) Can you name the Shakespeare play from this ultra short plot summary:
Friends arrange a match between one pair of lovers, and an enemy tries to break up another pair.

366) From which Shakespeare play is this line taken:
A fine volley of words, gentlemen,
And quickly shot off.

. . . Answers

356. Richard Brautigan

357. C.P. Snow

358. Willa Cather

359. "Anatomy of an Illness"

360. (Malvolio in) "Twelfth-Night"

361. Enid Bagnold

362. Richard Lovelace in "To Althea from Prison"

363. Incorrect, other way around

364. The American Civil War

365. "Much Ado About Nothing"

366. (Silvia in) "The Two Gentlemen of Verona"

367) An ex-football player makes big business of religion, according to Sinclair Lewis.

368) Creator of Perry Mason?

369) Name of F. Scott Fitzgerald's wife?

370) Frederick Rolfe, known as Baron _____ .

371) Even if you have not, like Keats, looked into Chapman's Homer, do you know Chapman's first name?

372) Two by Iris Murdoch: "An Unofficial _____ " and "A _____ Head."

373) "Ruggles of Red Gap" involves:
   a. life in a Devonshire public school
   b. the first British pilots in World War I
   c. an English butler in the old West

374) "Confessions of an English _____ _____ "?

375) British poet and artist was a friend of Thomas Paine and denounced George III and the King of France.

376) Charles Dickens left what novel unfinished at his death?

377) In Tolstoy's "War and Peace," who had to leave the outskirts of Moscow under difficult circumstances?

378) From which Shakespeare play is this line taken:
   She's beautiful and therefore to be woo'd;
   She is a woman, therefore to be won.

379) Correct or incorrect?
   The Prisoner of Zenda: Lord Byron
   The Prisoner of Chillon: Anthony Hope Hawkins

. . . Answers

367. "Elmer Gantry"

368. Erle Stanley Gardner

369. Zelda

370. Corvo

371. George

372. "An Unofficial Rose" and "A Severed Head"

373. c

374. "Confessions of an English Opium Eater"

375. William Blake

376. "The Mystery of Edwin Drood"

377. Napoleon and the French army

378. (Earl of Suffolk in) "First Part of King Henry VI"

379. Incorrect, other way around

380) British jockey turned bestselling writer?

381) Dostoevski's account of his prison years?

382) Correct or incorrect?
Jackie Collins: The Company of Women
Mary Gordon: Chances

383) From which Shakespeare play is this line taken:
By all the vows that ever men have broke,
In number more than ever women spoke . . .

384) Author of "If You Could See Me Now"?

385) Can you name the Shakespeare play from this ultra short plot summary:
A weak and unlikeable king alienates his people, is poisoned and succeeded by his son.

386) The famous opening sentence of Caesar's "Gallic Wars" states that all Gaul is divided into how many parts?

387) Yankee manager turned author?

388) From which Shakespeare play is this line taken:
And let not women's weapons, water-drops
Stain my man's cheeks!

389) Author of "Up from Slavery"?

390) What Frenchman claimed the following?
If God did not exist, it would be necessary to invent him.

391) Correct or incorrect?
Ruth Beebe Hill: Hanta Yo
Anna Lee Waldo: Sacajawea

. . . *Answers*

380. Dick Francis

381. "The House of the Dead"

382. Incorrect, other way around

383. (Hermia in) "A Midsummer-Night's Dream"

384. Peter Straub

385. "King John"

386. Three

387. Billy Martin

388. (Lear in) "King Lear"

389. Booker T. Washington

390. Voltaire

391. Correct

392) Name of family in "The Winds of War" and "War and Remembrance"?

393) When John Osborne and Kingsley Amis first appeared on the literary scene, they were known as what?

394) This diet doctor did not die of anorexia — he had a misunderstanding with a schoolmarm. His name and that of his book?

395) From which Shakespeare play is this line taken:
Uneasy lies the head that wears the crown.

396) Who wrote "An American Tragedy"?
   a. F. Scott Fitzgerald
   b. Theodore Dreiser
   c. H. L. Mencken
   d. Sherwood Anderson

397) Who was so pleased with "Alice's Adventures in Wonderland," she invited Lewis Carroll to dedicate his next book to her — which turned out to be a dry mathematics textbook?

398) Dostoevski's last novel?

399) From which Shakespeare play is this line taken:
Small have continual plodders ever won,
Save base authority from others' books.

400) Pip is told he will be the heir of an unknown benefactor and sets off for London, in which Dickens novel?

401) Italian author of "Conjugal Love" and "Two Women"?

402) Norman Mailer's story of an American infantry platoon hitting a Japanese-held Pacific island?

. . . Answers

392. Henry

393. Angry Young Men

394. Herman Tarnowner, M.D., "The Complete Scarsdale Medical Diet"

395. (King Henry in) "Second Part of King Henry IV"

396. b

397. Queen Victoria

398. "The Brothers Karamazov"

399. (Berowne in) "Love's Labour's Lost"

400. "Great Expectations"

401. Alberto Maravia

402. "The Naked and the Dead"

403) Howard Fast's book on the children of "The Immigrants"?

404) "The Metamorphoses" was written by:
   a. Catullus
   b. Virgil
   c. Julius Caesar
   d. Ovid

405) From which Shakespeare play is this line taken:
   Who woo'd in haste and means to wed at leisure

406) Henry Miller's letters to her were published in 1965 and her Diaries have aroused widespread interest.

407) Author of "Roots"?

408) Correct or incorrect?
   Aeschylus: Oedipus at Colonus
   Sophocles: The Seven Against Thebes

409) Popular title of the first edition of Shakespeare's collected plays and its date of publication?

410) "With No _____ ," title of Barry Goldwater's memoirs.

411) British author of "A Kid for Two Farthings" and "Expresso Bongo"?

412) Name of Tom Sawyer's aunt?

413) Malcolm Lowry's "Under the Volcano" is about:
   a. a pro tennis player
   b. a homosexual geologist
   c. an alcoholic consul
   d. a bored tour guide

. . . *Answers*

403. "Second Generation"

404. d

405. (Katharina in) "The Taming of the Shrew"

406. Anaïs Nin

407. Alex Haley

408. Incorrect, other way around

409. First Folio, 1623

410. "With No Apologies"

411. Wolf Mankowitz

412. Aunt Sally

413. e

414) Correct or incorrect?
   Petronius: Satyricon
   Cicero: De Senectute

415) Name the novels in the trilogy "U.S.A." by John Dos Passos.

416) Author of "Sonnets from the Portuguese"?

417) From which Shakespeare play is this line taken:
   Frailty, thy name is woman!

418) "The Amityville Horror" has a real location—where is Amityville?

419) Name of lawsuit in Dickens' "Bleak House"?

420) Correct or incorrect?
   Sam Shepard: True West
   Sam Beckett: Rockaby

421) What literary lion is a fabulous feline.

422) The first collection of Shakespeare plays left one play out which is generally believed to be his. Which play?

423) Four by Harold Robbins:
   "The _____ Merchants"
   "Where _____ Has Gone"
   "A _____ for Danny Fisher"
   "Never Love a _____ "

424) Think of computers and cutting up a page in order to rearrange words at random.

. . . *Answers*

414. Correct

415. "The 42nd Parallel," "1919" and "The Big Money"

416. Elizabeth Barrett Browning

417. (Hamlet in) "Hamlet"

418. Long Island, New York

419. Jarndyce vs. Jarndyce

420. Correct

421. Garfield

422. "Pericles"

423. "The Dream Merchants"
     "Where Love Has Gone"
     "A Stone for Danny Fisher"
     "Never Love a Stranger"

424. William S. Burroughs

425) From which Shakespeare play is this line taken:
  O! beware, my lord, of jealousy;
  It is the green-eyed monster that doth mock
  The meat it feeds on . . .

426) Author of "Lord Jim"?

427) From which Shakespeare play is this line taken:
  What's gone and what's past help
  Should be past grief . . .

428) What poet is associated with Amherst, Massachusetts?

429) Four by Alexander Solzhenitsyn:
  " _____ _____ in the Life of Ivan Denisovich"
  "Cancer _____ "
  "The _____ Circle"
  "The _____ Archipelago"

430) Murder in a 14th century Italian monastery, by Umberto Eco?

431) Author of "Darkness at Noon"?
  a. Zane Grey
  b. James T. Farrell
  c. Arthur Koestler
  d. Thornton Wilder

432) Edward Fitzgerald's translation of the "Rubaiyat of Omar Khayyam" proved to be:
  a. an original poem in English with little to do with the Persian original
  b. a much closer translation than at first believed

433) "When the hounds of spring are on winter's traces . . ." was written by?

. . . *Answers*

425. (Iago in) "Othello"

426. Joseph Conrad

427. (Paulina in) "The Winter's Tale"

428. Emily Dickinson

429. "One Day in the Life of Ivan Denisovich"
     "Cancer Ward"
     "The First Circle"
     "The Gulag Archipelago"

430. "The Name of the Rose"

431. c

432. b

433. Algernon Charles Swinburne

434) Who ordered these words to be placed where?
Cast a cold eye
On life, on death.
Horseman, pass by!

435) From which Shakespeare play is this line taken:
The evil that man do lives after them,
The good is oft interred with their bones . . .

436) Correct or incorrect?
Danielle Steel: A Perfect Stranger
Belva Plain: Random Winds

437) Who foretold the invention of submarines in what book featuring Captain Nemo?

438) From which Shakespeare play is this line taken:
Thou hast nor youth nor age,
But, as it were, an after-dinner's sleep,
Dreaming on both . . .

439) Name the five novels in The Leatherstocking Tales by James Fenimore Cooper.

440) Which of Poe's stories could be regarded as a forerunner of Melville's "Moby-Dick"?

441) An early episode in the life of Henry James involved a bicycle trip across India. True or false?

442) First name of Leopold Bloom's wife?

443) In which Dickens story does Little Nell appear?

. . . Answers

434. W.B. Yeats, on his own tombstone

435. (Antony in) "Julius Caesar"

436. Correct

437. Jules Verne in "Twenty Thousand Leagues Under the Sea"

438. (Vincentio, the Duke, in) "Measure for Measure"

439. "The Pioneers," "The Last of the Mohicans," "The Prairie," "The Pathfinder" and "The Deerslayer"

440. "The Narrative of A. Gordon Pym"

441. False

442. Molly

443. "The Old Curiosity Shop"

444) The person, the poem, the poet?
> She smiled, no doubt,
> Whene'er I passed her; but who passed without
> Much the same smile? This grew; I gave commands;
> Then all smiles stopped together. There she stands
> As if alive . . .

445) Pre-Raphaelite who placed a sheaf of poems in the casket of his loved one, and later had her exhumed when he found he had no copies?

446) Central character of "Wuthering Heights"?

447) Sir Walter Raleigh spoke these words to whom?
> What dost thou fear? Strike, man!

448) In Ionesco's play, the hero is afraid of remaining a human being while everyone else is turning into what?

449) From which Shakespeare play is this line taken:
> For there was never yet philosopher
> That could endure the tooth-ache patiently . . .

450) Inveterate enemy of Sherlock Holmes?

451) Mark Twain's real name?

452) Captain Hook, Tiger Lily and Tinker Bell are characters in what story?

453) Who did Barbara Frietchie confront with the Union flag?

454) Four by Longfellow:
> "The _____ of Miles Standish"
> " _____ of a Wayside Inn"
> "The Wreck of the _____ "
> "The _____ at Springfield"

. . . *Answers*

444. The late wife of the Duke of Ferrara, "My Last Duchess" by Robert Browning

445. Dante Gabriel Rossetti

446. Heathcliff

447. His executioner

448. Rhinoceroses

449. (Leonato in) "Much Ado About Nothing"

450. Moriarty

451. Samuel Langhorne Clemens

452. "Peter Pan"

453. Stonewall Jackson and his men

454. "The Courtship of Miles Standish"
     "Tales of a Wayside Inn"
     "The Wreck of the Hesperus"
     "The Arsenal at Springfield"

455) Private detective Mike Hammer appears in what writer's stories?

456) Creator of Gargantua and Pantagruel?

457) Author of "Buddenbrooks"?
   a. Rainer Maria Rilke
   b. Hermann Hesse
   c. Thomas Mann
   d. Heinrich Boll

458) From which Shakespeare play is the line taken:
   As flies to wanton boys, are we to the gods;
   They kill us for their sport.

459) Who was the compiler of "An American Dictionary of the English Language" (1828)?

460) Daniel Defoe's "Robinson Crusoe" was a work of fiction based on what real person's adventures?

461) In Waugh's "Brideshead Revisited," Charles _____ met Sebastian _____ at Oxford.

462) From which Shakespeare play is this line taken:
   Zounds! I was never so bethumped with words
   Since I first call'd my brother's father dad.

463) What was Lemuel Gulliver's occupation?

464) Real name of O. Henry?

465) "The Red Badge of Courage" dealt with what war?

466) English author's mechanical citrus fruit?

. . . *Answers*

455. Mickey Spillane's

456. Rabelais

457. c

458. (Earl of Gloucester in) "King Lear"

459. Noah Webster

460. Alexander Selkirk's

461. Charles Ryder, Sebastian Marchmain

462. (The bastard in) "King John"

463. Ship's physician

464. William Sydney Porter

465. The American Civil War

466. Anthony Burgess' "Clockwork Orange"

467) Author of "Strictly from Hunger," "Westward Ha!" and "The Rising Gorge"?

468) Title of the play which claims Mozart was murdered by another composer?

469) How many of Shakespeare's plays were published in his lifetime?

470) "The White-Boned Demon" by Ross Terrill is about:
   a. Madame Mao Zedong
   b. Charles Darwin
   c. Michael Jackson
   d. Arnold Palmer

471) Creator of "Don Quixote"?

472) Robbe-Grillet, Sarraute, Resnais, Godard and Truffaut belong to what cultural movement?

473) Spell the fictional county associated with William Faulkner. It begins with a Y.

474) Can you name the Shakespeare play from this ultra short plot summary:
   Very young king and the intrigues at court.

475) What city, seen from what bridge, by what poet?
   Ships, towers, domes, theatres, and temples lie
   Open unto the fields, and to the sky;
   All bright and glittering in the smokeless air.

476) Five by William Faulkner:
   "The _____ and the Fury"
   " _____ in the Dust"
   "Requiem for a _____ "
   "The Wild _____ "
   "King's _____ "

. . . Answers

467. S.J. Perelman

468. "Amadeus"

469. 18

470. a

471. Cervantes

472. The New Wave (La Nouvelle Vague)

473. Yoknapatawpha

474. "Part One of Henry VI"

475. London, from Westminster Bridge, by William Wordsworth

476. "The Sound and the Fury"
"Intruder in the Dust"
"Requiem for a Nun"
"The Wild Palms"
"King's Gambit"

477) Goliardic verse was often impolite student and minstrel verse in Latin. True or false?

478) He wrote the libretto for Richard Strauss' "Der Rosenkavalier":
    a. August Heinrich Hoffmann
    b. Hugo von Hofmannsthal
    c. Christian Hofmann von Hofmannswaldau

479) To hide from his fame, what last name did Lawrence of Arabia assume as a private in the RAF?

480) Can you name the Shakespeare play from this ultra short plot summary:
    After numerous reverses on the battlefield, where the ex-queen is more in evidence than the ex-king, the king is executed in the Tower.

481) In Kafka's "Metamorphosis," the hero awakes one morning to find himself turned into what?

482) Don Quixote's squire?

483) From which Shakespeare play is this line taken:
    The quality of mercy is not strain'd,
    It droppeth as the gentle rain from heaven
    Upon the place beneath . . .

484) "Jane Eyre" and "Wuthering Heights" were written by different Brontë sisters. True or false?

485) Author of the Ragged Dick Series and Luck and Pluck Series?

486) The woods are lovely, dark and deep,
    But I have promises to keep,
    And . . .?

. . . *Answers*

477. True

478. b

479. Shaw

480. "Part Three of Henry VI"

481. A huge insect

482. Sancho Panza

483. (Portia in) "The Merchant of Venice"

484. True

485. Horatio Alger, Jr.

486. And miles to go before I sleep,
    And miles to go before I sleep.

487) Title of Nathanael West's Hollywood novel?

488) What does the E. E. stand for in E. E. Cummings?

489) Bestselling "60 Minutes" author?

490) Can you name the Shakespeare play from this ultra short plot summary:
   The King of England successfully invades France.

491) Correct or incorrect?
   Hart Crane: The Bridge
   Stephen Crane: The Red Badge of Courage

492) Dr. Seuss' "The Cat in the _____ ."

493) The author of "An Indecent Obsession" also wrote:
   a. "Fear and Loathing on the Campaign Trail"
   b. "Surrender to Love"
   c. "The Cardinal Sins"
   d. "The Thornbirds"

494) One was an extravagant tipper, one moderate, one a hardliner. Which was which?
   Balzac
   Dickens
   Proust

495) Three by Thomas Hardy: "The Mayor of _____ ," "The Return of the _____ " and "Jude the _____ ."

496) Compiler of the anthology "The Golden Treasury"?

. . . *Answers*

487. "The Day of the Locust"

488. Edward Estlin

489. Andy Rooney

490. "King Henry V"

491. Correct

492. "The Cat in the Hat"

493. d

494. Proust, extravagant; Balzac, moderate; Dickens, a hardliner

495. "The Mayor of Casterbridge," "The Return of the Native" and "Jude the Obscure"

496. Francis Turner Palgrave

497) "Dead Souls" was written by:
   a. Gogol
   b. Dostoevsky
   c. Gorki
   d. Tolstoy

498) What major Russian author died in a small railroad station?

499) How many sonnets did Shakespeare publish in his famous sequence?

500) From which Shakespeare play is this line taken:
   Some Cupid kills with arrows, some with traps.

501) In Greek it is Homer's "Iliad," in Latin it is Virgil's _____ ?

502) Who wrote "Oh Dad, Poor Dad, Mama's Hung You in the Closet and I'm Feeling So Sad"?

503) Alice meets the: _____ Rabbit
   _____ Hatter
   _____ Cat
   _____ Hare
   _____ Turtle

504) Which of Dostoevski's "Brothers Karamazov" is accused of their father's murder?
   a. Dmitri
   b. Ivan
   c. Alyosha

505) From which Shakespeare play is this line taken:
   There's small choice in rotten apples

. . . *Answers*

497. a

498. Leo Tolstoy

499. 154

500. (Hero in) "Much Ado About Nothing"

501. "Aeneid"

502. Arthur Kopit

503. White Rabbit, Mad Hatter, Cheshire Cat, March Hare, Mock Turtle

504. a

505. (Hortensio in) "The Taming of the Shrew"

QUESTIONS

506) Two by Margaret Mead: "Coming of Age in _____ " and "Growing Up in _____ _____ ."

507) Who wrote these lines?
I'm Smith of Stoke, aged sixty-odd,
I've lived without a dame
From youth-time on; and would to God
My dad had done the same.

508) "Aztec" and "The Journeyer" were written by:
a. Gary Jennings
b. Howard Fast
c. Martin Cruz Smith
d. Belva Plain

509) "Sons and _____ ."

510) Correct or incorrect?
666: Jay Anson
XPD: Len Deighton

511) Shakespeare's son's name?

512) " _____ Sandwiches," name of book by Allen Ginsberg.

513) From which Shakespeare play is this line taken:
It is a wise father that knows his own children.

514) Poet and poem?
What seas what shores what granite islands towards my timbers
And woodthrush calling through the fog
My daughter.

515) Robert Penn Warren has denied that Willie Stark in "All the King's Men" is based on what Louisiana politician?

. . . Answers

506. "Coming of Age in Samoa" and "Growing Up in New Guinea"

507. Thomas Hardy

508. a

509. "Sons and Lovers"

510. Correct

511. Hamnet

512. "Reality Sandwiches"

513. (Launcelot Gobbo in) "The Merchant of Venice"

514. T.S. Eliot, "Marina"

515. Huey Long

516) Real name of Flann O'Brien aka Myles na gCopaleen?

517) Can you name the Shakespeare play from this ultra short plot summary:
   The duke leaves the city in charge of a deputy but stays on in disguise to see what will happen.

518) Humorist who helped found a publishing house?

519) The famous tavern of Prince Hal and Sir John Falstaff?

520) Norman Mailer helped free him from jail, with an unfortunate result. Name the writer and his book.

521) "SS-GB" and "Berlin Game" are by:
   a. Eric Ambler
   b. Len Deighton
   c. Alistair McClean
   d. Ken Follett

522) Name of Travis McGee's boat?

523) Who wrote these lines?
   The cow is of the bovine ilk;
   One end is moo, the other, milk.

524) Can you name the Shakespeare play from this ultra short plot summary:
   He will avenge his father's murder, or maybe he won't.

525) "Pain Erasure: The Bonnie Prudden Way" — real book or just a notion?

. . . *Answers*

516. Brian Nolan

517. "Measure for Measure"

518. Bennett Cerf co-founded Random House in 1927

519. Boar's Head Tavern

520. Jack Abbott, "In the Belly of the Beast"

521. b

522. The Busted Flush

523. Ogden Nash

524. "Hamlet"

525. Real book, published in 1982

QUESTIONS

26) "The Orphan Angel" by Elinor Wylie is about what might have happened:
   a. if Shelley had been rescued from drowning by an American ship
   b. If Icarus had not lost his wings
   c. if Napoleon had been crowned King of England

27) Name the first American novel of the sea and its author.

28) In his later years, Milton suffered from what major physical handicap?

29) Where was the elderly Dr. Johnson persuaded to go on a walking tour?

30) What famous novel ends with the words " . . . and yes said yes I will Yes"?

31) Three by Joseph Wambaugh: " _____ and Shadows," "The _____ Field" and "The _____ Dome."

32) Economist's book which first brought up the concepts of "conspicuous leisure" and "conspicuous consumption"?

33) Can you name the Shakespeare play from this ultra short plot summary:
   A man exiled from the English court bets with another man that his wife is faithful and is tricked into believing she is not.

34) Name of the lady the Great Gatsby pines for?

35) Who wrote these lines?
   Success is counted sweetest
   By those who ne'er succeed.

. . . *Answers*

526. a

527. "The Pilot" (1823) by James Fenimore Cooper

528. Blindness

529. The Hebrides or western isles of Scotland

530. "Ulysses" by James Joyce

531. "Lines and Shadows," "The Onion Field" and "The Glitter Dome"

532. "The Theory of the Leisure Class" by Thorstein Veblen

533. "Cymbeline"

534. Daisy Buchanan

535. Emily Dickinson

536) "The Cannibal," "The Lime Twig" and "Second Skin" are by?

537) Can you name the Shakespeare play from this ultra short plot summary:
   A man disillusioned by his friends goes off to live in a cave and bargains with a general to attack the city.

538) From which Shakespeare play is this line taken:
   Britain is
   A world by itself, and we will nothing pay
   For wearing our own noses

539) What American poet withheld his name from the title page of his first book, instead appearing in a photograph and describing himself as "turbulent, fleshy, sensual, eating, drinking and breeding"?

540) What character in a book said this of his author?
   He told the truth, mainly. There was things which he stretched, but mainly he told the truth.

541) Who wrote "The Rime of the Ancient Mariner"?

542) The N.Y. Times described this bestseller as "the erotic side of the Japanese samurai tradition." Title and author?

543) Irish short story writer who spent much of his adult life in Brooklyn?

544) Two of these are by the Editors of Playgirl. Which two?
   a. "Overcoming the Fear of Success"
   b. "Cheeks"
   c. "The New Women's Guide to Getting Married"
   d. "Hunks"

. . . *Answers*

536. John Hawks

537. "Timon of Athens"

538. (Cloten in) "Cymbeline"

539. Walt Whitman in the first edition of "Leaves of Grass," printed in Brooklyn in 1855

540. Huck Finn

541. Samuel Taylor Coleridge

542. "The Ninja" by Eric Van Lustbader

543. Frank O'Connor

544. b, d

545) Can you name the Shakespeare play from this ultra short plot summary:

The king and three friends swear to devote themselves to study and avoid romance — until a princess and her three friends arrive.

546) Who wrote "Of Human Bondage"?

547) Name Ichabod Crane's rival who masqueraded as the headless horseman.

548) What college did Longfellow attend as a student in America?

549) Peter Matthiessen tramped about the Himalayas in search of what feline?

550) Can you name the Shakespeare play from this ultra short plot summary:

An upstanding man joins conspirators to kill a dictator.

551) True story of millionaire's daring rescue of his men from Iran by the author of "The Eye of the Needle."

552) Two are friends but unfriendly with the third. Which is odd man out?
   a. William F. Buckley
   b. Norman Mailer
   c. Gore Vidal

553) From which Shakespeare play is this line taken:
If it were done when 'tis done, then 'twere well
It were done quickly . . .

554) Which well known American critic and fiction writer did not file his federal income tax returns from 1946 to 1955?

. . . *Answers*

545. "Love's Labour's Lost"

546. W. Somerset Maugham

547. Brom Bones

548. Bowdoin

549. "The Snow Leopard"

550. "Julius Caesar"

551. "Wings of Eagles" by Ken Follett

552. c

553. (Macbeth in) "Macbeth"

554. Edmund Wilson

555) John Kennedy Toole's "A Confederacy of _____ ."

556) What was Thomas Hardy before he became a writer?

557) Three by Vladimir Nabakov:
"Invitation to a _____ "
"Laughter in the _____ "
" _____ Sinister"

558) "As I Lay _____ " by William Faulkner.

559) Can you name the Shakespeare play from this ultra short plot summary:
The king's ne'er-do-well son defeats Hotspur and the rebels.

560) "Rebecca," "Frenchman's Creek," "My Cousin Rachel," "The Breaking Point" . . . who wrote them?

561) From which Shakespeare play is this line taken:
A countenance more in sorrow than in anger.

562) Arthur Miller and Tennessee Williams collaborated as young men on an uncompleted play on the digging of the Erie Canal. True or false?

563) "What Color Is Your Parachute?" deals with:
a. job hunting and career changing
b. commercial airliner safety
c. new fashion ideas
d. becoming a mercenary

564) The real identity of the writer of "Shibumi" has never been revealed. His pen name is?

. . . *Answers*

555. "A Confederacy of Dunces"

556. An architect

557. "Invitation to a Beheading"
     "Laughter in the Dark"
     "Bend Sinister"

558. "As I Lay Dying"

559. "Part One of Henry IV"

560. Daphne du Maurier

561. (Horatio in) "Hamlet"

562. False

563. a

564. Trevanian

565) Author of "While Reagan Slept"?
   a. Art Buchwald
   b. F. Mondale
   c. Theodore Sorenson
   d. William Manchester

566) Picasso's ex-mistress turned author, much to the great man's discontent.

567) "Moviola," set in Hollywood, was written by:
   a. William Goldman
   b. Joseph Wambaugh
   c. Eve Babbitt
   d. Garson Kanin

568) Shakespeare's birthplace?

569) What American novelist left an 8-foot-high manuscript when he died suddenly?

570) Can you name the Shakespeare play from this ultra short plot summary:
   The queen of the Goths and her sons are brought as prisoners to Rome and are soon involved in murder, rape and mayhem.

571) "Blood Wedding" by Eudora Welty is about:
   a. a Florida Gulf Coast fishing community
   b. a 1940s Southern plantation family
   c. a toreador and an American nurse
   d. a woman's drive to marry a banker's son

572) In Hemingway's "Old Man and the Sea," what kind of fish does the old man catch and what ultimately happens to it?

573) Playwright of "The Maids," "The Balcony" and "The Blacks"?

. . . *Answers*

565. a

566. Françoise Gilot, who wrote "Life with Picasso" with Carlton Lake

567. d

568. Stratford-on-Avon

569. Thomas Wolfe

570. "Titus Andronicus"

571. b

572. An enormous marlin, which is later devoured by sharks except for its skeleton

573. Jean Genet

574) "Utterly Gross _____ " by Julius Alvin.

575) In Arthur Miller's play "Death of a Salesman," what was the salesman's name?

576) Putters-together of lists: Irving, David, Amy and Sylvia?

577) Official U.S. Navy historian during World War II, his books deal with New England and war at sea. His name?

578) Can you name the Shakespeare play from this ultra short plot summary:
   A man marries and attempts to control a strong-willed woman.

579) "Serpentine" and "Celebrity" are by:
   a. Thomas Thompson
   b. Irwin Shaw
   c. Tom Wicker
   d. William Goldman

580) Correct or incorrect?
   C. S. Forester: A Passage to India
   E. M. Forster: The African Queen

581) Two by Erma Bombeck: "Aunt Erma's _____ Book" and " _____ The Second Oldest Profession."

582) Name of Thomas Mann's confidence trickster?

583) Three by Sigmund Freud:
   "Totem and _____ "
   "The Ego and the _____ "
   "Moses and _____ "

. . . *Answers*

574. "Utterly Gross Jokes"

575. Willy Loman

576. Wallace/Wallechinsky

577. Samuel Eliot Morison

578. "The Taming of the Shrew"

579. a

580. Incorrect, other way around

581. "Aunt Erma's Cope Book" and "Motherhood: The Second Oldest Profession"

582. Felix Krull

583. "Totem and Taboo"
"The Ego and the Id"
"Moses and Monotheism"

584) "The Anatomy of Melancholy" was published by 1621. Who wrote it?
    a. Robert Burton
    b. Sir Walter Raleigh
    c. Christopher Marlowe
    d. Ben Jonson

585) From which Shakespeare play is this line taken:
Beauty provoketh thieves sooner than gold.

586) A long poem by William Carlos Williams is called after what New Jersey city?

587) Stephen King wrote these:
"Salem's _____ "
"The Dead _____ "
"Pet _____ "

588) A couple whose troubles made recent literature:
    a. Milton and Rose Friedman
    b. P. D. James and John Le Carré
    c. Nora Ephron and Carl Bernstein
    d. Maxine Hong Kingston and James Clavell

589) Correct or incorrect?
Oliver Wendell Holmes, Sr.: Elsie Venner
Oliver Wendell Holmes, Jr.: The Common Law

590) Three by Irving Wallace:
"The Seven _____ "
"The Nympho and _____ _____ "
"The _____ Document"

591) Jack Gelber's play about junkies

. . . *Answers*

584. a

585. (Rosalind in) "As You Like It"

586. Paterson

587. "Salem's Lot," "The Dead Zone," "Pet Semetary"

588. c

589. Correct

590. "The Seven Minutes," "The Nymphs and Other Mani
acs," "The R Document"

591. "The Connection"

592) Leading Russian-born composer who late in life wrote books in English in collaboration with an American conductor?

593) British man-of-letters long resident on the island of Majorca?

594) "A Man Called Intrepid" was written by:
   a. Len Deighton
   b. William Stevenson
   c. Barbara W. Tuchman
   d. Leslie A. Marchand

595) The critic who married Vanessa Stephen, sister of Virginia Woolf?

596) "The Shadow of a Gunman," "Juno and the Paycock" and "The Plough and the Stars" are by?

597) From which Shakespeare play is this line taken:
   Friends, Romans, countrymen, lend me your ears . . .

598) Shaw named two contemporary authors "the Chesterbelloc." Who were they?

599) Author of the Forsyte Saga?

600) From which Shakespeare play is this line taken:
   Though this be madness, yet there is method in't.

601) Edith Sitwell believed she was a reincarnation of Catherine de Medici. True or false?

602) From which Shakespeare play is this line taken:
   Full fathom five thy father lies;
   Of his bones are coral made;
   These are the pearls that were his eyes . . .

. . . *Answers*

592. Igor Stravinsky, with Robert Craft

593. Robert Graves

594. b

595. Clive Bell

596. Sean O'Casey

597. (Antony in) "Julius Caesar"

598. G.K. Chesterton and Hilaire Belloc

599. John Galsworthy

600. (Polonius in) "Hamlet"

601. False, she just liked to wear medieval dress

602. (Ariel in) "The Tempest"

603) Name of scholar on whose literal translations from the Chinese and Japanese Ezra Pound depended?

604) Last name of the poor student who commits murder in Dostoevski's "Crime and Punishment"?

605) Author of "The Four Just Men" and "Sanders of the River"?

606) Where was Shaw's play "The Devil's Disciple" set?

607) "Porgy," DuBose Heyward's novel and later play — later still the basis of an opera — was set along what street in what town?

608) Correct or incorrect?
    Thucydides: History of the Peloponnesian War
    Xenophon: Anabasis

609) Names of books by James A. Michener set in the following locations?
    a. South Africa
    b. Spain
    c. Maryland
    d. Colorado

610) The bitter satire "A Modest Proposal" suggested that the poor raise their children to be sold, butchered and eaten. Who was its author?

611) Name of William F. Buckley's superspy?

612) From which Shakespeare play is this line taken:
    It is the curse of kings to be attended
    By slaves that take their humours for a warrant . . .

. . . Answers

603. E.F. Fenollosa

604. Raskolnikov

605. Edgar Wallace

606. In America during the Revolution

607. Catfish Row, Charleston, SC

608. Correct

609. a) "The Covenant," b) "Iberia," c) "Chesapeake," d) "Centennial"

610. Jonathan Swift

611. Blackford Oakes

612. (King John in) "King John"

613) What kind of highways did William Least Heat Moon write about?

614) Did Sinclair Lewis win the Nobel Prize for Literature?

615) Correct or incorrect?
Sherwood Anderson: The Petrified Forest
Robert E. Sherwood: Dark Laughter

616) How many books in Homer's "Iliad"?
   a. 4
   b. 13
   c. 24
   d. 35

617) First name of Joan Crawford's author daughter?

618) "The Body _____ " by Victoria.

619) Who wrote "Winesburg, Ohio"?
   a. Maxwell Anderson
   b. Robert W. Anderson
   c. Sherwood Anderson

620) "The Diary of Anne Frank" was first published in English under what title?

621) "Ordinary People" was written by:
   a. Judith Krantz
   b. Jacqueline Briskin
   c. Judith Guest
   d. Joyce Haber

622) Who wrote these words?
For fools rush in where angels fear to tread.

623) Wil _____ created "Gnomes."

. . . *Answers*

613. "Blue Highways"

614. Yes, in 1930

615. Incorrect, other way around

616. c

617. Christina

618. Principal

619. c

620. "The Diary of a Young Girl"

621. c

622. Alexander Pope

623. Huygen

624) Modern pop music group has name of 1925 John Dos Passos novel.

625) The sage of Concord?

626) From which Shakespeare play is this line taken:
Is she worth keeping? why, she is a pearl,
Whose price hath launched above a thousand ships,
And turn'd crown'd kings to merchants.

627) Two by John D. MacDonald: "The _____ Ripper" and "The Empty _____ Sea."

628) From which Shakespeare play is this line taken:
Fortune brings in some boats that are not steer'd.

629) Name of the family in Steinbeck's "The Grapes of Wrath"?

630) Later name of LeRoi Jones?

631) Why lower-case a and m for archy and mehitabel?

632) Author and champion of black magic and witchcraft, he was a model for Somerset Maugham's "The Magician."

633) Author of "The Dragons of Eden"?
   a. Isaac Asimov
   b. Carl Sagan
   c. Arthur C. Clarke
   d. Frank Herbert

634) Who was the real Poor Richard of the Almanacs?

635) Name of Mr. O'Hara's plantation?

. . . *Answers*

624. "Manhattan Transfer"

625. Ralph Waldo Emerson

626. (Troilus in) "Troilus and Cressida"

627. "The Green Ripper" and "The Empty Copper Sea"

628. (Pisanio in) "Cymbeline"

629. Joad

630. Amiri Baraka

631. Because archy did his own typing and could not operate the shift key on the typewriter

632. Aleister Crowley

633. b

634. Benjamin Franklin

635. Tara

636) "A Distant Mirror" was about life in what century?
   a. 11th
   b. 14th
   c. 16th
   d. 18th

637) Emily _____, author of "Etiquette."

638) In Steinbeck's "The Grapes of Wrath," the family moved from what state to what state?

639) "Gravity's Rainbow" and "V." were written by?

640) Can you name the Shakespeare play from this ultra short plot summary?
   Two lovers escape to the forest and meet the king and queen of the fairies.

641) The Greenwich Village bar where Dylan Thomas downed his last whiskies?

642) Author of the libretto for the musical "Show Boat"?

643) "Cold Comfort Farm" (1932) by Stella Gibbons was:
   a. an account of an eccentric girlhood on a great estate
   b. a satire on grim rural novels in Hardy's tradition
   c. the life of a woman country doctor that influenced Herriot
   d. a description of collective agriculture in the U.S.S.R.

644) "The Color Purple" by Alice Walker is about:
   a. Daughters of the American Revolution
   b. life in 3000 A.D.
   c. new decor approach
   d. black women in the South

. . . *Answers*

636. b

637. Post

638. Oklahoma to California

639. Thomas Pynchon

640. "A Midsummer-Night's Dream"

641. The White Horse Tavern

642. Oscar Hammerstein, 2nd

643. b

644. d

645) Real name of Genet, author and New Yorker correspondent in Paris for many years?

646) Who wrote "A Tree Grows in Brooklyn"?
   a. Betty Smith
   b. Thomas Wolfe
   c. Clare Boothe Luce
   d. Francine du Plessix Gray

647) Pilot author of "Flight to Arras" and "The Little Prince"?

648) French author of "Madame Bovary"?

649) "Quo Vadis?," the novel set in Nero's Rome, was originally written in what language?

650) In whose memory were these lines written by W.H. Auden?
   The brooks were frozen, the airports almost deserted,
   And snow disfigured the public statues . . .
   The day of his death was a dark cold day.

651) Play by Arthur Miller about the Salem witchcraft trials?

652) His famous schoolbooks — the Readers and Speller — sold more than 100 million copies. His last name?

653) From which Shakespeare play is this line taken:
   This royal throne of kings, this sceptre isle . . .
   This other Eden, demi-paradise . . .
   This blessed plot, this earth, this realm, this England.

654) The animal-loving doctor hero of Hugh Lofting's children's stories?

655) Creator of Barry Lyndon?

. . . *Answers*

645. Janet Flanner

646. a

647. Antoine de Saint-Exupéry

648. Gustave Flaubert

649. Polish

650. W.B. Yeats

651. "The Crucible"

652. McGuffey

653. (John of Gaunt in) "King Richard II"

654. Dr. Doolittle

655. William Makepeace Thackeray

656) Playwright, politician, ambassador, wife of publisher Henry R.?

657) From Columbus, Ohio, he was hailed in New York for his funny stories and drawings but said to be a mean drunk. Who?

658) Author of "Thy Neighbor's wife"?
   a. William F. Buckley
   b. Gay Talese
   c. Nancy Friday
   d. Norman Mailer

659) From which Shakespeare play is this line taken:
   We are stuff
   As dreams are made on, and our little life
   Is rounded with a sleep.

660) From which Shakespeare play is this line taken:
   All the world's a stage,
   And all the men and women merely players . . .

661) As the patient improves, the psychiatrist worsens . . . Name of this psychiatrist in Fitzgerald's "Tender Is the Night"?

662) Can you name the Shakespeare play from this ultra short plot summary:
   A pleasant but ineffectual king is overthrown by Bolingbroke.

663) Author of Portnoy's Complaint?

664) Name and author of bestseller about life in the year 3000, written by a cult leader whose son claimed is being held captive by his followers?

... *Answers*

656. Clare Boothe Luce

657. James Thurber

658. b

659. (Prospero in) "The Tempest"

660. (Jacques in) "As You Like It"

661. Dick Diver

662. "Richard II"

663. Philip Roth

664. "Battlefield Earth" by L. Ron Hubbard

665) From which Shakespeare play is this line taken:
How sharper than a serpent's tooth it is
To have a thankless child!

666) The 1800 novel "Castle Rackrent" was written by Maria _____ ?

667) Shakespeare stole at least one plot from him. He in turn called William an "upstart crow," before dying "of a surfeit of pickled herring and Rhenish wine." His name?

668) Who gave New York City the name Gotham?

669) Real identity of Buck Mulligan in Joyce's "Ulysses"?
   a. Charles Stewart Parnell
   b. Oliver St. John Gogarty
   c. George Moore
   d. Padraic Colum

670) Name of writer who speared Ernest in "Portrait of Hemingway" and wrote account of John Huston filming "The Red Badge of Courage"?

671) Correct or incorrect?
Father Brown: Lewis Carroll
Father William: G.K. Chesterton

672) From which Shakespeare play is this line taken:
When love begins to sicken and decay,
It useth an enforced ceremony.

673) Colombian author of "One Hundred Years of Solitude"?

674) Title of Edgar Rice Burroughs's first Tarzan book and its date of publication?

. . . Answers

665. (Lear in) "King Lear"

666. Edgeworth

667. Robert Greene

668. Washington Irving in his 1807 "Salmagundi Papers"

669. b

670. Lillian Ross

671. Incorrect, other way around

672. (Brutus in) "Julius Caesar"

673. Gabriel Garcīa Márquez

674. "Tarzan of the Apes" (1914)

675) He wrote the text for Handel's "Ode for St. Cecilia's Day"
   a. John Donne
   b John Dryden
   c. Alexander Pope
   d. George Herbert

676) Amy _____ smoked big black cigars.

677) Who wrote these lines?
   Hope is the thing with feathers
   That perches in the soul . . .

678) Name the volumes in the Studs Lonigan trilogy.

679) Virginia Woolf took her own life:
   a. with a bullet
   b. by poison
   c. by drowning
   d. by none of the above

680) How did Dr. Johnson define his own profession — lexicographer — in his dictionary?

681) In Homer's "Iliad," Hector kills Patroclus and he in turn is killed by:
   a. Achilles
   b. Agamemnon
   c. Priam
   d. Briseis

682) Name of private eye in Hammett's "The Maltese Falcon"?

. . . Answers

675. b

676. Lowell

677. Emily Dickinson

678. "Young Lonigan," "The Young Manhood of Studs Lonigan," "Judgment Day"

679. c

680. One who compiles dictionaries. A harmless drudge.

681. a

682. Sam Spade

683) A biographer complained that a life of Walter Pater was nearly impossible to write because Pater:
    a. invented so many wildly improbable tales about himself
    b. so rarely took an active part in anything
    c. required his friends to swear they would reveal nothing about him

684) From which Shakespeare play is this line taken:
    He lives in fame that died in virtue's cause.

685) Can you name the Shakespeare play from this ultra short plot summary:
    Twin brothers search for each other.

686) Four travel books by D.H. Lawrence:
    "Twilight in _____"
    "Sea and _____"
    "Mornings in _____"
    "_____ Places"

687) Author of the novel "Show Boat"?

688) What descends from the sky in James Joyce's famous short story "The Dead"?

689) Popular TV talk show host used his last name as the title of his book. What was it?

690) Yorkshire veterinarian.

691) From which Shakespeare play is this line taken:
    For we may pity, though not pardon thee.

692) Who wrote of Katherine Hepburn in a play that her acting ran "the whole gamut of emotions from A to B"?

. . . Answers

683. b

684. (Group in) "Titus Andronicus"

685. "The Comedy of Errors"

686. "Twilight in Italy"
"Sea and Sardinia"
"Mornings in Mexico"
"Etruscan Places"

687. Edna Ferber

688. Snow

689. "Donahue"

690. James Herriot

691. (Solinus, Duke of Ephesus, in) "The Comedy of Errors"

692. Dorothy Parker

693) Can you name the Shakespeare play from this ultra short plot summary·

A twin brother and sister have been separated, and when the sister dresses as a pageboy, confusion results.

694) Author of "Jacob's Room"?

695) Name the four stories contained in Edith Wharton's "Old New York."

696) Author of "Pale Horse, Pale Rider"?

697) Who ate the flowers of a narcotic plant that induced lassitude and contentment?

698) Indian author of "Gone Away"?

699) From which Shakespeare play is this line taken:

I think the king is but a man, as I am: the violet smells to him as it doth to me . . .

700) Welsh national congress of bards — spell it.

701) Connecticut insurance executive who wrote poetry in his spare time?

702) "The Eagles Gather" and "The Turnbulls" were written by Erskine Caldwell or Taylor Caldwell?

703) In which play did Tom Conti win a Tony for his portrayal of a sculptor paralyzed from the neck down?

704) From which Shakespeare play is this line taken:

O powerful love! that, in some respects, makes a beast of man; in some other, a man a beast.

... *Answers*

693. "Twelfth-Night"

694. Virginia Woolf

695. "False Dawn," "The Old Maid," "The Spark" and "New Year's Day"

696. Katherine Anne Porter

697. The Lotus-Eaters

698. Dom Moraes

699. (King Henry in) "King Henry V"

700. Eisteddfod

701. Wallace Stevens

702. Taylor Caldwell

703. "Whose Life Is It Anyway?"

704. (Sir John Falstaff in) "The Merry Wives of Windsor"

705) Correct or incorrect?
   Ben Jonson: Comus
   John Milton: Volpone

706) What ending do Rupert Brooke, Edward Thomas and Wilfrid Owen share in common?

707) Who wrote the hardboiled 1930s novel "The Postman Always Rings Twice"?
   a. Ross McDonald
   b. Dashiell Hammett
   c. Mickey Spillane
   d. James M. Cain

708) Name the poet and the poem which begins:
   I do not know much about gods; but I think that the river
   Is a strong brown god — sullen, untamed and intractable
   . . .

709) Title of James Baldwin's first novel?

710) From which Shakespeare play is this line taken:
   I had rather hear my dog bark at a crow than a man swear he loves me.

711) Humphrey Chimpden Earwicker's initials are important in what work?

712) Correct or incorrect?
   Mrs. Dalloway: Jan Struther
   Mrs. Miniver: Virginia Woolf

713) From which Shakespeare play is this line taken:
   So wise so young, they say, do never live long.

714) "Out of the Cradle Endlessly Rocking" — whose title?

. . . Answers

705. Incorrect, other way around

706. They died in World War I

707. d

708. T.S. Eliot, "The Dry Salvages," third of the Four Quartets

709. "Go Tell It on the Mountain"

710. (Beatrice in) "Much Ado About Nothing"

711. "Finnegan's Wake"

712. Incorrect, other way around

713. (Richard as Duke of Gloucester in) "King Richard III"

714. Walt Whitman's

715) "The _____ and Daniel Webster," Stephen Vincent Benét's short story.

716) In Waugh's "A Handful of Dust," what does the mad old man force the hero to do every afternoon?

717) First a TV script, then a movie script, about a lonely Bronx butcher who meets an unmarried schoolteacher. Title and writer?

718) Titles of the two volumes of Carl Sandburg's "Abraham Lincoln"?

719) Don Quixote's horse?

720) Goethe's early novel "The Sorrows of Young Werther" caused what reaction among its young male readers?

721) From which Shakespeare play is this line taken:
    You taught me language; and my profit on't
    Is, I know how to curse.

722) Sequel to Milton's "Paradise Lost"?

723) Author of "The Magnificent Ambersons"?

724) "Grace Abounding to the Chief of Sinners" (1666) was an autobiography by a man known for a more famous work. That work and his name?

725) Sarah Gamp and Seth Pecksniff are in which Dickens story?

726) Creator of Christopher Robin and Winnie-the-Pooh?

727) "Our Town," "The Skin of Our Teeth" and "The Matchmaker" are plays by?

. . . *Answers*

715. "The Devil and Daniel Webster"

716. Read Dickens aloud

717. "Marty" by Paddy Chayevsky

718. Vol. 1: "The Prairie Years"; vol. 2: "The War Years"

719. Rocinante

720. A wave of suicides

721. Caliban in "The Tempest"

722. "Paradise Regained"

723. Booth Tarkington

724. "Pilgrim's Progress," John Bunyan

725. "The Life and Adventures of Martin Chuzzlewit"

726. A.A. Milne

727. Thornton Wilder

728) "Color Me Beautiful" by Carole Jackson is about:
   a. watercolor painting
   b. beauty tips for women
   c. house decorating
   d. Cabbage Patch dolls

729) Gordon Ashe, Michael Halliday, Jeremy York and J. J. Marric are all pen names for what British author?

730) From which Shakespeare play is this line taken:
   Good night, sweet prince,
   And flights of angels sing thee to thy rest!

731) John O'Hara set many of his novels and stories in what fictitious town in what real state?

732) "Nightwood" was written by _____ Barnes.

733) Name the country of giants twelve times the size of man in "Gulliver's Travels."

734) Name of Tom Sawyer's sweetheart?

735) Brendan Behan's first play?

736) Sir Winston Churchill was awarded the Nobel Prize for Literature. True or False?

737) According to Robert Frost, one could do worse than be . . . what?

738) Virginia, Leonard, Lytton, Roger and Bertrand belonged to what group?

739) The hero of Sinclair Lewis's "Dodsworth" was a wealthy automobile manufacturer in what Midwestern city?

. . . Answers

728. b

729. John Creasey

730. (Horatio in) "Hamlet"

731. Gibbsville, PA

732. Djuna

733. Brobdingnag

734. Becky Thatcher

735. "The Quare Fellow"

736. True, in 1953

737. A swinger of birches

738. The Bloomsbury group

739. Zenith

740) From which Shakespeare play is this line taken:
Age cannot wither her, nor custom stale
Her infinite variety . . .

741) Sports writer turned short story writer, from teens through thirties, with a perfect ear for the conversational styles of baseball players and barbers?

742) Correct or incorrect?
Richard Henry Dana, Sr.: The Idle Man
Richard Henry Dana, Jr.: Two Years Before the Mast

743) Budd Schulberg's version of F. Scott Fitzergerald's Hollywood days?

744) Famed British translator of Chinese and Japanese poetry?

745) "Megatrends" by John Naisbitt is about:
a. a vitamin scandal
b. new weight loss methods
c. America in the next decade
d. Detroit car designs

746) "Imprisoned in every fat man," wrote what British critic about himself, "a thin one is wildly signalling to be let out"?

747) John Ford, William Rowley and Thomas Dekker wrote:
a. biblical commentary
b. an encyclopedia of herbal remedies
c. accounts of travels abroad
d. plays

748) Donne, Herbert, Crashaw, Cleveland, Marvell and Cowley are known as what?

. . . *Answers*

740. (Enobarbus in) "Antony and Cleopatra"

741. Ring Lardner

742. Correct

743. "The Disenchanted"

744. Arthur Waley

745. c

746. Cyril Connolly

747. d

748. The metaphysical poets or school

49) From which Shakespeare play is this line taken:
Sweet mercy is nobility's true badge . . .

50) Title of Waugh's satire on Hollywood morticians?

51) Correct or incorrect?
Christopher Marlowe: The Jew of Malta
Thomas Kyd: The Spanish Tragedy

52) The lover of the Roman poet Catullus held what pet at
er breast?

53) Fantasy writer and a peer?

54) One of the Cambridge critics and a defender of D.H.
Lawrence:
a. F.R. Leavis
b. Malcolm Muggeridge
c. Kenneth Tynan

55) George Orwell, author of "1984," served with the Impe-
ial Police in what Asian country?

56) Correct or incorrect?
Of Time and the River: John Steinback
Of Mice and Men: Thomas Wolfe

57) What was archy, and mehitabel?

58) A. J. Liebling was expelled from Dartmouth College for
hat reason?

59) From which Shakespeare play is this line taken:
Cowards die many times before their deaths;
The valiant never taste of death but once.

. . . *Answers*

749. (Tamora in) "Titus Andronicus"

750. "The Loved One"

751. Correct

752. A sparrow

753. Lord Dunsany

754. a

755. Burma

756. Incorrect, other way around

757. archy, a cockroach; mehitabel, a cat

758. For refusing to attend chapel

759. (Julius Caesar in) "Julius Caesar"

60) Four by F. Scott Fitzgerald:
"The _____ Gatsby"
"_____ Is the Night"
"This _____ of Paradise"
"The _____ Tycoon"

61) The term Shangri-La is from James Hilton's "Lost Horizon." Hilton wrote what better known book?

62) In Shaw's play, what was "Mrs. Warren's Profession"?

63) From which Shakespeare play is this line taken:
Could I come near your beauty with my nails
I'd set my ten commandments in your face.

64) Author of "Guys and Dolls"?

65) Correct or incorrect?
Plato: Dialogues
Aristotle: Poetics

66) Katherine Mansfield wrote:
a. plays
b. novels
c. short stories
d. screenplays

67) From what play, by what playwright?
But when I call to mind I am a king,
Methinks I should revenge me of my wrongs,
That Mortimer and Isabel have done.

68) From which Shakespeare play is this line from:
Men at some time are masters of their fates:
The fault, dear Brutus, is not in our stars,
But in ourselves, that we are underlings.

. . . *Answers*

760. "The Great Gatsby"
     "Tender Is the Night"
     "This Side of Paradise"
     "The Last Tycoon"

761. "Goodbye, Mr. Chips"

762. Prostitution

763. (Eleanor, Duchess of Gloucester, in) "Second Part of King Henry VI"

764. Damon Runyon

765. Correct

766. c

767. "Edward the Second" by Christopher Marlowe

768. (Cassius in) "Julius Caesar"

769) Author of "Ivanhoe"?

770) Mary McCarthy was associated in the 1930s and 1940s with which one of these magazines:
    a. Hudson Review
    b. Partisan Review
    c. New Yorker
    d. Atlantic Monthly

771) From which Shakespeare play is this line taken:
    Yet my good will is great, though the gift small.

772) Correct or incorrect?
    The Man Who Was: Rudyard Kipling
    The Man Who Was Thursday: G.K. Chesterton

773) Author of "Tobacco Road" and "God's Little Acre"?

774) Denizen of Greenwich Village, he and his wife were found murdered.

775) "Happy Days," "Newspaper Days" and "Heathen Days" are the three volumes of whose autobiography?

776) There are several guides to this type of young Southern California female, called a _____?

777) Herman Melville and Nathaniel Hawthorne were close friends. True or false?

778) Laurence Sterne began an account of whose "life story" with his conception and ended it with his birth?

779) From which Shakespeare play is this line taken:
    Rumour doth double, like the voice and echo,
    The numbers of the fear'd.

. . . *Answers*

769. Sir Walter Scott

770. b

771. Thaisa in "Pericles"

772. Correct

773. Erskine Caldwell

774. Maxwell Bodenheim

775. H.L. Mencken's

776. Valley girl

777. True

778. "Tristam Shandy"

779. The Earl of Warwick in "Second Part of King Henry IV"

QUESTIONS

780) Shakespeare's daughters' names?

781) Shaw's "Major Barbara" held that rank in what organization?

782) Who was the author and what was the title of the book that had the following subtitle?
Who was Born in Newgate, and during a Life of continu'd Variety for Threescore Years, besides her Childhood, was Twelve Year a Whore, five times a Wife (whereof once to her own Brother), Twelve Year a Thief, Eight Year a Transported Felon in Virginia, at last grew Rich, liv'd Honest, and died a Penitent, Written from her own Memorandums . . .

783) The "Playboy riots" took place in Dublin in 1908 and later in New York and Philadelphia over what play by what playwright?

784) From which Shakespeare play is this line taken:
Marry, he must have a long spoon that must eat with the devil.

785) Correct or incorrect:
Harold Robbins: The Key to Rebecca
Ken Follett: Goodbye Janette

786) "Peter Quince at the Clavier" was written by:
a. William Carlos Williams
b. Ezra Pound
c. T. S. Eliot
d. Wallace Stevens

787) Three by Carson McCullers:
"The Heart Is a _____ _____"
"Reflections in a _____ _____"
"The Ballad of the _____ _____"

143

. . . Answers

780. Susanna and Judith

781. The Salvation Army

782. Daniel Defoe, "The Fortunes and Misfortunes of the Famous Moll Flanders"

783. "The Playboy of the Western World" by J.M. Synge

784. (Dromio of Syracuse in) "The Comedy of Errors"

785. Incorrect, other way around

786. d

787. "The Heart Is a Lonely Hunter"
"Reflections in a Golden Eye"
"The Ballad of the Sad Cafe"

788) Correct or incorrect?
   Ross McDonald: Travis McGee
   John D. MacDonald: Lew Archer

789) Lilac time: name the two poets who wrote these lines.
   a. April is the cruellest month, breeding Lilacs out of the
      dead land . . .
   b. When lilacs last in the dooryard bloom'd . . .

790) What these people have to say is not always what is on
their headstones in that graveyard. Where is the graveyard?

791) "Little Gloria . . . Happy at Last" — Gloria who?

792) With words by James Agee and photos by Walker
Evans, what was the title of this study of Alabama sharecrop-
pers during the Depression?

793) 1930s travel book on Iran (Persia) in which the then
shah is mockingly referred to as Marjoribanks?

794) From which Shakespeare play is this line taken:
   Some rise by sin, and some by virtue fall . . .

795) First name of Henry James' philosopher-writer brother?

796) Angela Lansbury, Brooke Adams and Phoebe Cates
starred in the ABC TV miniseries based on which book by
Shirley Conran?

797) Correct or incorrect?
   A Room of One's Own: Virginia Woolf
   A Room With a View: E. M. Forster

798) Correct or incorrect?
   D. H. Lawrence: Seven Pillars of Wisdom
   T. E. Lawrence: The Rainbow

. . . Answers

788. Incorrect, other way around

789. a) T.S. Eliot; b) Walt Whitman

790. Spoon River

791. Vanderbilt

792. "Let Us Now Praise Famous Men"

793. "The Road to Oxiana" by Robert Byron

794. (Escalus in) "Measure for Measure"

795. William

796. "Lace"

797. Correct

798. Incorrect, other way around

799) Name a children's book by a famous 20th century spy novelist.

800) "Lady Chatterley's Lover" was what on her husband's estate?

801) "Golden Boy" and "The Country Girl" are by what playwright?

802) Harold Ross, James Thurber, Wilcott Gibbs, S. J. Perelman and E. B. White were associated with what magazine?

803) From which Shakespeare play is this line taken:
    That man that hath a tongue, I say, is no man,
    If with his tongue he cannot win a woman.

804) Russian author who used titles such as "The Bedbug" and "The Cloud in Trousers"?

805) Leigh Brackett, Larry Niven and Alan Dean Foster all write what kind of fiction?

806) Countee _____.

807) Ernest Hemingway, E.E. Cummings and John Dos Passos all did what when?

808) From which Shakespeare play is this line taken:
    There's beggary in the love that can be reckon'd.

809) Author of "The Informer"?

810) Hitler's autobiography?

811) W. Somerset Maugham's novel based on the life of the painter Paul Gauguin?

. . . *Answers*

799. "Chittychittybangbang" by Ian Fleming

800. Gamekeeper

801. Clifford Odets

802. "The New Yorker"

803. (Valentine in) "The Two Gentlemen of Verona"

804. Vladimir Mayakovsky

805. Science fiction

806. Countee Cullen

807. Served in the Norton-Harjes Ambulance Service during World War I

808. (Antony in) "Antony and Cleopatra"

809. Liam O'Flaherty

810. "Mein Kampf" ("My Struggle")

811. "The Moon and Sixpence"

812) Who wrote "The Man With the Golden Arm"?
   a. Nelson Algren
   b. Sinclair Lewis
   c. John Steinbeck
   d. James T. Farrell

813) From which Shakespeare play is this line taken:
   When Fortune means to men most good,
   She looks upon them with a threatening eye.

814) American literary critic who was also a fan of the desert and nature?

815) Name of the powerful white trader in Conrad's "Heart of Darkness"?

816) Gulley Jimson was its hero.

817) English playwright who wrote "The Winslow Boy" and "Separate Tables"?

818) Tell Jeeves to inform the Honourable Bertie Wooster that one is a friend of what author?

819) From which Shakespeare play is this line taken:
   Our remedies oft in ourselves do lie
   Which we ascribe to heaven . . .

820) From which Shakespeare play is this line taken:
   Let me have men about me that are fat;
   Sleek-headed men and such as sleep o' nights.
   Yond Cassius has a lean and hungry look;
   He thinks too much: such men are dangerous.

821) In Wolfe's "Look Homeward, Angel," the town of Altamont in Catawba state is said to be what real town in what real state?

. . . Answers

812. a

813. Pandulph in "King John"

814. Joseph Wood Krutch

815. Kurtz

816. "The Horse's Mouth"

817. Terence Rattigan

818. P.G. Wodehouse

819. Parolles in "All's Well That Ends Well"

820. (Julius Caesar in) "Julius Caesar"

821. Asheville, NC

QUESTIONS

822) Two by Dee Brown: "Bury My _____ at Wounded _____" and "Creek Mary's _____."

823) J. R. R. Tolkien's last?

824) Who wrote the passage that contains these words?
No man is an island. . . . Never send to know for whom the bell tolls; it tolls for thee.

825) "Mr. Britling Sees It Through" and "The History of Mr. Polly" are by?

826) "The Bee Gees' Book of Aerobic Dancing" — real book or just a notion?

827) Collection of short pieces by the host of "The Prairie Home Companion" radio show?

828) In Hemingway's "For Whom the Bell Tolls," what is the American hero's task?

829) Author of "Some Fruits of Solitude"?
a. Cotton Mather
b. Henry David Thoreau
c. William Penn
d. Richard Henry Dana, Sr.

830) Hero of "The Catcher in the Rye"?

831) The play "Our Town" is set where?

832) Roald _____ writes macabre stories.

833) From which Shakespeare play is this line taken:
Or is the adder better than the eel
Because his painted skin contents the eye?

. . . Answers

822. "Bury My Heart at Wounded Knee" and "Creek Mary's Blood"

823. "The Silmarillion"

824. John Donne

825. H.G. Wells

826. Just a notion

827. "Happy to Be Here"

828. To blow up a bridge

829. c

830. Holden Caulfield

831. Grover's Corners, NH

832. Dahl

833. (Petruchio in) "The Taming of the Shrew"

834) Name the two theatres in which Shakespeare was a part owner.

835) Name the only extant trilogy of classical Greek plays, the playwright and the plays.

836) From which Shakespeare play is this line taken:
Better a little chiding than a great deal of heart-break.

837) F. Scott Fitzgerald's name for the 1920s?

838) Can you name the Shakespeare play from this ultra short plot summary:
A Roman causes trouble at home by dallying on the Nile.

839) From which Shakespeare play is this line taken:
Something is rotten in the state of Denmark.

840) Author of "King Solomon's Mines"?

841) In Poe's "The Fall of the House of Usher," what happened to the actual house in the end?

842) Subtitle of Lewis Carroll's "Through the Looking-Glass"?

843) Actor author of "The Moon Is a Balloon"?

844) Robert H. Schuller would recognize which one of the following as a colleague?
a. Edward I. Koch
b. Joseph Wambaugh
c. Erma Bombeck
d. Billy Graham

. . . Answers

834. The Globe and Blackfriars

835. The Oresteia by Aeschylus: "Agamemnon," "The Choëphoroe" and "The Eumenides"

836. (Mistress Page in) "The Merry Wives of Windsor"

837. The Jazz Age

838. "Antony and Cleopatra"

839. (Marcellus in) "Hamlet"

840. Rider Haggard

841. It split asunder and sank into the tarn

842. "And What Alice Found There"

843. David Niven

844. d

845) "Gather ye rose-buds while ye may" was the advice of:
   a. Robert Herrick
   b. George Herbert
   c. Alexander Pope
   d. John Dryden

846) Harold Gray's 20th century comic strip "Little Orphan Annie" got its title from what, by whom?

847) The Hartford Wits were also known as what?

848) Creator of "Little Lord Fauntleroy"?

849) A blade attached to a pendulum swings back and forth, moving closer to the body of a bound prisoner . . . Name of story, and of author?

850) On attaining the rank of major-general, Ulysses S. Grant destroyed all surviving copies of a private printing of his love poems. True or false?

851) Frazer's "The Golden Bough" was composed of:
   a. translations from Chinese poetry
   b. comparative religion and mythology
   c. the reveries of an opium addict
   d. history and tradition of European banks

852) Henry Miller's trip to Greece?

853) Poet who read at John F. Kennedy's presidential inauguration?

854) From which Shakespeare play is this line taken:
   Out of this nettle, danger, we pluck this flower, safety.

855) The author of "Tom Jones" was associated with the Bow Street runners. Who were they?

. . . Answers

845. a

846. The dialect poem "Little Orphant Annie" by James Whitcomb Riley

847. The Connecticut Wits or the Yale Poets

848. Frances Hodgson Burnett

849. "The Pit and the Pendulum," Edgar Allan Poe

850. False, he never printed or perhaps even wrote any, though he did complete his "Personal Memoirs," which became a posthumous bestseller

851. b

852. "The Colossus of Maroussi"

853. Robert Frost

854. (Hotspur in) "First Part of King Henry IV"

855. The early police force; in 1749 Henry Fielding became London's first police magistrate

856) In 1982 two books on how to play Pac Man sold more than a million copies each. True or false?

857) Dumas pere's "The Man in the Iron Mask" is based on a real person. True or false?

858) "Finnegan's _____."

859) Name poet and poem for his mother:
Caw caw caw crows shriek in the white sun over grave stones in Long Island . . .

860) Correct or incorrect?
Paul Theroux: In Patagonia
Bruce Chatwin: The Old Patagonian Express

861) English humorist and expert on gamesmanship, life-manship and one-upmanship?

862) From which Shakespeare play is this line taken:
There are more things in heaven and earth, Horatio,
Then are dreamt of in your philosophy.

863) "Mrs. Wiggs of the Cabbage Patch" was published in 1901. What was the Cabbage Patch?

864) From which Shakespeare play is this line taken:
It is a tale
Told by an idiot, full of sound and fury,
Signifying nothing.

865) Frenchman more interested in flowers of evil than leaves of grass.

866) Dame Rose Macaulay's bizarre trip to Turkey?

. . . Answers

856. True

857. True, he was jailed for more than 40 years but probably was not the king's brother

858. "Finnegan's Wake"

859. Allen Ginsberg, "Kaddish"

860. Incorrect, other way around

861. Stephen Potter

862. (Hamlet in) "Hamlet"

863. A collection of shacks by the railroad in a Kentucky town

864. (Macbeth in) "Macbeth"

865. Charles Baudelaire

866. "The Towers of Trebizond"

QUESTIONS

867) George Lucas is credited as author of the book "Star Wars." True or false?

868) Jacobo Timerman's "Prisoner Without a _____, Cell Without a _____."

869) From which Shakespeare play is this line taken:
   To mourn a mischief that is past and gone
   Is the next way to draw new mischief on.

870) Russian author of "Eugene Onegin" and "Boris Godunov"?

871) "Getting _____" by Woody Allen.

872) James Joyce wrote a play. True or false?

873) An English lord who wrote, swam and loved incomparably?

874) "In Search of Excellence" and "Up the Organization" are about:
   a. grass-roots politics
   b. business corporations
   c. presidential primaries
   d. organized religion

875) Correct or incorrect?
   Aristophanes: Iphigenia in Aulis
   Euripides: The Frogs

876) Creator of Gunga Din?

877) From which Shakespeare play is this line taken:
   Ay, every inch a king:
   When I do stare, see how the subject quakes.

. . . Answers

867. True

868. "Prisoner Without a Name, Cell Without a Number"

869. (Duke of Venice in) "Othello"

870. Alexander Pushkin

871. "Getting Even"

872. True, "Exiles"

873. Byron

874. b

875. Incorrect, other way around

876. Rudyard Kipling

877. (Lear in) "King Lear"

QUESTIONS

878) Alfred Jarry wrote "Ubu Roi." True or false?

879) In "The Hunchback of Notre Dame," what was the bellringer's name?

880) Shakespeare's mother's name?

881) Which Athenian philosopher tutored Alexander the Great?

882) French author of "Nana"?

883) Can you name the Shakespeare play from this ultra short plot summary:
    An envious man tricks a general into believing his wife is unfaithful to him and he strangles her.

884) "A High Wind in Jamaica" centered on:
    a. eccentricities in a colonial men's club
    b. children captured by pirates
    c. an uprising of plantation workers
    d. Caribbean yacht racing

885) "The Boys from Brazil" was written by:
    a. Gerald Green
    b. Graham Greene
    c. Ira Levin
    d. Julio Cortazar

886) Can you name the Shakespeare play from this ultra short plot summary:
    Husband, wife and daughter are shipwrecked, separated and find each other after years have passed.

. . . *Answers*

878. True

879. Quasimodo

880. Mary Arden

881. Aristotle

882. Emile Zola

883. "Othello"

884. b

885. c

886. "Pericles"

887) Creator of "Elegy in a Country Churchyard"?
    a. Wordsworth
    b. Gray
    c. Shelley
    d. Keats

888) Uriah Heep is a villain in which Dickens story?

889) "The Rolling Stone"—not the rock magazine, but the original magazine published in Austin, Texas, from 1894 to 1895—was published by whom?

890) Can you name the Shakespeare play from this ultra short plot summary:
    An uncompromising Roman, driven from the city, returns to attack it but is persuaded by his wife and mother to lift his siege.

891) Oscar Wilde's "The Importance of Being _____."

892) Author of "Dragonsong," "Dragonsinger" and "Dragondrums"?

893) Correct or incorrect?
    Janet Dailey: No Time for Tears
    Cynthia Freeman: Nightway

894) Can you name the Shakespeare play from this ultra short plot summary:
    During a truce in the Trojan War, a Trojan prince loses his loved one to a Greek.

895) Max Reiner is the occasional pen name of what popular female American author?

896) Psychoanalyst author of "Listening With the Third Ear" and "The Need to be Loved"?

. . . *Answers*

887. b

888. "David Copperfield"

889. O. Henry

890. "Coriolanus"

891. "The Importance of Being Earnest"

892. Anne McCaffrey

893. Incorrect, other way around

894. "Troilus and Cressida"

895. Taylor Caldwell

896. Theodor Reik

897) The musical "My Fair Lady" was based on what play by what playwright?

898) The New York City hotel with bronze plaques to some of the many writers who have lived there?

899) Four by Aldous Huxley:
  "Antic _____"
  "_____ Counter _____"
  "Chrome _____"
  Brave _____ _____"

900) From which Shakespeare play is this line taken:
  Self-love, my liege, is not so vile a sin
  As self-neglecting.

901) Can you name the Shakespeare play from this ultra short plot summary:
  Girl disguised as boy in the forest has some romantic confusions.

902) Correct or incorrect?
  Truman Capote: The Executioner's Song
  Norman Mailer: In Cold Blood

903) "The Journal of Albion Moonlight" and "Memoirs of a Shy Pornographer" — who wrote them?

904) New York writer killed by a dune buggy while sleeping on the beach at Fire Island?

905) Paul Gallico's charwoman?

906) V.C. Andrews wrote terror stories about what family?

907) How many plays is Shakespeare generally credited with today?

. . . Answers

897. "Pygmalion" by George Bernard Shaw

898. Chelsea Hotel

899. "Antic Hay," "Point Counter Point," "Chrome Yellow," "Brave New World"

900. (Lewis, the Dauphin, in) "King Henry V"

901. "As You Like It"

902. Incorrect, other way around

903. Kenneth Patchen

904. Frank O'Hara

905. Mrs. 'Arris

906. Dollanganger

907. 37

908) Oh, to be in England
Now that _____ there . . .

909) "None of my relations ever spoke to me of my books. . . . The subject was avoided as if it were a kind of family disgrace, which might be condoned but could not be forgotten." Which of these authors?
   a. Henry James
   b. Edith Wharton
   c. Gertrude Stein
   d. F. Scott Fitzgerald

910) Correct or incorrect?
   Moss Hart: The Man Who Came to Dinner
   Bret Harte: Outcasts of Poker Flat

911) Title of William L. Shirer's history of Nazi Germany?

912) Can you name the Shakespeare play from this ultra short plot summary:
   The king is dominated by the queen and a duke, and rebellion breaks out.

913) Beat author of "On the Road"?

914) Founder of the Dada movement in Paris?

915) Russian author of "The Lower Depths"?

916) Isaac Asimov is the pen name of three New York University professors. True or false?

. . . Answers

908. April's

909. b

910. Correct

911. "The Rise and Fall of the Third Reich"

912. "Part Two of King Henry VI"

913. Jack Kerouac

914. Tristan Tzara

915. Maxim Gorki

916. Very false

QUESTIONS

917) Who wrote this in the introduction to his classic book, called what, about a desert?

You can't see *anything* from a car; you've got to get out of the goddamned contraption and walk, better yet crawl, on your hands and knees, over the sandstone and through the thornbush and cactus. When traces of blood begin to mark your trail you'll see something, maybe. Probably not.

918) Can you name the Shakespeare play from this ultra short plot summary:

The king tries to have his marriage annuled but meets some opposition.

919) Louis Auchincloss's stories deal with:
   a. the old West
   b. merchant seamen
   c. the upper echelons of society
   d. the newspaper world

920) From which Shakespeare play is this line taken:
The fool doth think he is wise, but the wise man knows himself to be a fool.

921) Robert Louis Stevenson spent months living in an abandoned house at what disused California mine?
   a. Yellow Astor
   b. Grass Valley
   c. Mother Lode
   d. Silverado

922) From which Shakespeare play is this line taken:
God give them wisdom that have it; and those that are fools, let them use their talents.

. . . Answers

917. Edward Abbey, "Desert Solitaire"

918. "Henry VIII"

919. c

920. (Touchstone in) "As You Like It"

921. d, he published an account of his stay there as "The Silverado Trail"

922. (Clown in) "Twelfth-Night"

923) In Homer's "Iliad," only one enlisted man, or regular soldier, in the Greek army is mentioned by name. What is his name?

924) Author of "The Bastard," "The Lawless" and "The Warriors"?

925) Longfellow's Acadian heroine?

926) The second half of Shakespeare's sonnets were addressed to a woman known as what?

927) "Jackie Oh!" was written by Mario Puzo. True or false?

928) Name of David Halberstam's book on the L.A. Times, Washington Post, Time Inc. and CBS?

929) Who wrote the words, Gilbert or Sullivan?

930) Can you name the Shakespeare play from this ultra short plot summary:
    Boy and girl and warring families.

931) "On a Grecian Urn," "On Melancholy" and "To a Nightingale" are all what kind of poem?

932) "Desire Under the Elms" was written by:
    a. Sean O'Casey
    b. W. B. Yeats
    c. Tennessee Williams
    d. Eugene O'Neill

933) Austrian writer Franz Werfel hid from the Nazis in a French church and later wrote a book celebrating that church's saint. Name of book?

934) From which Shakespeare play is this line taken:
Cry 'Havoc!' and let slip the dogs of war . . .

... *Answers*

923. Thersites

924. John Jakes

925. Evangeline

926. The Dark Lady

927. False, it was written by Kitty Kelley

928. "The Powers That Be"

929. Gilbert

930. "Romeo and Juliet"

931. Odes

932. d

933. "The Song of Bernadette"

934. (Antony in) "Julius Caesar"

935) From which Shakespeare play is this line taken:
Ill blows the wind that profits nobody.

936) Reviver of Arts and Crafts Movement whose wallpapers are better remembered than his words today?

937) From which Shakespeare play is this line taken:
All that glistens is not gold . . .

938) From which Shakespeare play is this line taken:
If you prick us, do we not bleed? if you tickle us, do we not laugh? if you poison us, do we not die? and if you wrong us, shall we not revenge? If we are like you in the rest, we will resemble you in that.

939) Who said the following?
There is nothing, Sir, too little for so little a creature as man.

940) "Sweet Afton" conjures up what name?

941) Can you name the Shakespeare play from this ultra short plot summary:
Two friends compete for the daughter of the duke.

942) French poet who was original campaigner for Cubist painting?

943) Who wished it said of him after he was gone?
He held his pen in trust
To art, not serving shame or lust.
a. Alfred, Lord Tennyson
b. Francis Thompson
c. Lionel Johnson
d. Austin Dobson

. . . Answers

935. (A son that has killed his father, in) "Third Part of King Henry VI"

936. William Morris

937. (The Prince of Morocco in) "The Merchant of Venice"

938. (Shylock in) "The Merchant of Venice"

939. Dr. Johnson

940. Robert Burns

941. "The Two Gentlemen of Verona"

942. Guillaume Apollinaire

943. d

944) Irving Stone's "Lust for Life" and "The Agony and the Ecstacy" were about what two artists?

945) Famous American war correspondent, killed near Okinawa, who published "Here Is Your War" and "Brave Men"?

946) John Steinbeck's effort on the biblical story of Cain and Abel?

947) From which Shakespeare play is this line taken:
The gods are just, and of our pleasant vices
Make instruments to plague us . . .

948) Book and author on which Roman Polanski's film "Tess" was based?

949) They thought the movie would help John Glenn win the 1984 presidential nomination — the movie didn't work but the book was a bestseller. Its title and author?

950) Can you give the *full* names of these 1930s London poets from their initials?
C. D. L.
L. McN.
S. S.
W. H. A.

951) "The Mabinogion" is a collection of tales translated from the medieval:
a. Finnish
b. Welsh
c. Wendish
d. Icelandic

952) George Eliot wrote "The Mill on the _____" and "Silas _____."

. . . Answers

944. Vincent van Gogh and Michelangelo

945. Ernie Pyle

946. "East of Eden"

947. (Edgar in) "King Lear"

948. "Tess of the d'Urbervilles" by Thomas Hardy

949. Thomas Wolfe, "The Right Stuff"

950. Cecil Day Lewis, Louis McNiece, Stephen Spender, Wystan Hugh Auden

951. b

952. "The Mill on the Floss," "Silas Marner"

953) Who wrote the screenplays for "All the President's Men" and "A Bridge Too Far"?

954) From which Shakespeare play is this line taken:
Conscience is but a word that cowards use,
Devis'd at first to keep the strong in awe:
Our strong arms be our conscience, swords our law.

955) "The Lives of a Cell" was written by:
a. Lewis Thomas
b. Carl Sagan
c. Isaac Asimov
d. Jane Fonda

956) Can you name the Shakespeare play from this ultra short plot summary:
A businessman borrows money with an IOU for a pound of his flesh.

957) Creator of "The Owl and the Pussycat"?

958) The publisher offered a $10,000 prize to the reader who submitted the best answer to the mystery raised in this bestseller — nothing to do with a gold rodent.

959) Nationality of the principal character in "Death in Venice"?

960) A little red book of quotations?

961) Famous English writer (1811-1863), born in India, dropped out of Cambridge, tried reading for law, abandoned painting in Paris, before trying his luck with the pen?

. . . Answers

953. William Goldman

954. (King Richard in) "King Richard III"

955. a

956. "The Merchant of Venice"

957. Edward Lear

958. "Who Killed the Robins Family?"

959. German

960. "Quotations from Chairman Mao Tsetung"

961. William Makepeace Thackeray

962) Can you name the Shakespeare play from this ultra short plot summary:

The king suspects his queen of having an affair with a friend and imprisons or exiles all concerned.

963) Ford Madox Ford's "Some Do Not," "No More Parades," "A Man Could Stand Up" and "The Last Post" were gathered under what single title?

964) Creator of "The Beggar's Opera"?

965) Author of "Bold Breathless Love," "Rash Reckless Love" and "Wild Willful Love"?
   a. Rosemary Rogers
   b. Valerie Sherwood
   c. Kathleen Woodiwiss

966) Shakespeare's wife's name?

967) Two by Lawrence Sanders: "The _____ of Peter S." and "The Third _____ _____."

968) "Kinflicks" was written by:
   a. Judy Blume
   b. Susan Isaacs
   c. Lisa Alther
   d. Erica Jong

969) Can you name the Shakespeare play from this ultra short plot summary:

He gave his kingdom to two daughters and nothing to the third, the only one who loved him.

970) Correct or incorrect?
   Dumas père: The Count of Monte Cristo
   Dumas fils: La Dame aux Camélias

. . . Answers

962. "The Winter's Tale"

963. "Parade's End"

964. John Gay

965. b

966. Anne Hathaway

967. "The Seduction of Peter S." and "The Third Deadly Sin"

968. c

969. "King Lear"

970. Correct

971) Correct or incorrect?
  Plain Language from Truthful James: Rudyard Kipling
  Plain Tales from the Hills: Bret Harte

972) After Shakespeare had become successful, he bought a large house in his birthplace. What is the name of this house?

973) Neil Simon wrote which of these plays?
  a. "Noises Off"
  b. "Torch Song Trilogy"
  c. "Brighton Beach Memoirs"
  d. "Glengarry Glen Ross"

974) Can you name the Shakespeare play from this ultra short plot summary:
  A lecherous knight tries to seduce two ladies.

975) "The Bridge of San Luis Rey" was written by:
  a. Ernest Hemingway
  b. Tennessee Williams
  c. William Carlos Williams
  d. Thornton Wilder

976) Author of the essay "A Dissertation on Roast Pig"?

977) What was the Ancient Mariner's crime?

978) Ellery Queen is the pen name of two men. True or false?

979) Who wrote the lyrics for "The Harp That Once Through Tara's Halls" and "The Minstrel Boy"?

980) What was the gypsy dancer's name in "The Hunchback of Notre Dame"?

981) John Cheever's "Chronicle" and "Scandal"?

... *Answers*

971. Incorrect, other way around

972. New Place

973. c

974. "The Merry Wives of Windsor"

975. d

976. Charles Lamb

977. He shot an albatross

978. True, Frederic Dannay and Manfred B. Lee

979. Thomas Moore

980. Esmeralda

981. "The Wapshot Chronicle," "The Wapshot Scandal"

982) The Newbery Medal is awarded annually for the best children's book written by an American. Who was Newbery?

983) "I will never live for the sake of another man, nor ask any other man to live for mine" is the philosophy of a new society being built by the characters of what novel by what author?

984) Author of "Nevada!" and "Wyoming!"?

985) Author of "Gulliver's Travels"?

986) Author of "The Joy of Sex":
   a. Nancy Friday
   b. Alex Comfort
   c. Gay Talese
   d. Xaviera Hollander

987) How did Odysseus' wife Penelope delay the suitors who wanted to marry her?

988) Author of "A Pair of Blue Eyes"?

989) "Tegucigalpa" was James A. Michener's first book. True or false?

990) British writer and mathematician whose life ranged from tea with the Bloomsbury set to campaigning for nuclear disarmament through civil disobedience. His name?

991) Many of her novels are set in the ancient Mediterranean, such as "The Last of the Wine," "The King Must Die" and "The Bull from the Sea." Her name?

... Answers

982. John Newbery (1713-1767), English publisher of newspapers and children's books

983. "Atlas Shrugged" by Ayn Rand

984. Dana Fuller Ross

985. Jonathan Swift

986. b

987. She promised to marry one of them as soon as she had finished weaving a shroud and by night she unraveled what she wove by day

988. Thomas Hardy

989. False, he hasn't written one with this title

990. Bertrand Russell

991. Mary Renault

992) "Return of the Druses," an account of this people in Syria and Lebanon, was written by:
   a. Percy Bysshe Shelley
   b. Lord Byron
   c. Alfred, Lord Tennyson
   d. Robert Browning

993) Correct or incorrect?
   A Portrait of the Artist as a Young Man: James Joyce
   A Portrait of the Artist as a Young Dog: Dylan Thomas

994) The doings of Serjeant Buzfuz, Messrs. Dodson and Fogg, Augustus Snodgrass, Samuel Weller and Nathaniel Winkle are revealed in what Dickens book?

995) Shakespeare's birth and death dates?

996) Studio insider who wrote "What Makes Sammy Run?" and "The Harder They Fall"?

997) "Good-bye to All That" was written by:
   a. Aldous Huxley
   b. Robert Graves
   c. George Orwell
   d. D. H. Lawrence

998) Who wrote "Songs of Innocence" and "Songs of Experience"?

999) Can you name the Shakespeare play from this ultra short plot summary:
   The hunchbacked and malignant king confiscates Bolingbroke's inheritance, is imprisoned and murdered.

1000) Sparky Lyle's book about the New York Yankees?

1001) Shaw's play "Androcles and the _____."

. . . Answers

992. d

993. Correct

994. "The Pickwick Papers"

995. 1564-1616

996. Budd Schulberg

997. b

998. William Blake

999. "Richard III"

1000. "The Bronx Zoo"

1001. "Androcles and the Lion"

QUESTIONS

1002) Boris Pasternak was awarded the Nobel Prize for Literature but was forced by the Soviet government to reject it. True or false?

1003) Correct or incorrect?
   John G. Fuller: Dynasty
   Robert S. Elegant: The Ghost of Flight 401

1004) He hated modern life and lived with hawks in the California mountains. His name?

1005) Two by Dashiell Hammett: "The _____ Key" and "The _____ Man."

. . . *Answers*

1002. True

1003. Incorrect, other way around

1004. Robinson Jeffers

1005. "The Glass Key" and "The Thin Man"

SENSATIONAL SAGAS!

WHITE NIGHTS, RED DAWN   (1277, $3.95)
by Frederick Nolan
Just as Tatiana was blossoming into womanhood, the Russian Revolution was overtaking the land. How could the stunning aristocrat sacrifice her life, her heart and her love for a cause she had not chosen? Somehow, she would prevail over the red dawn —and carve a destiny all her own!

IMPERIAL WINDS   (1324, $3.95)
by Priscilla Napier
From the icebound Moscow river to the misty towers of the Kremlin, from the Bolshevick uprising to the fall of the Romanovs, Daisy grew into a captivating woman who would courageously fight to escape the turmoil of the raging IMPERIAL WINDS.

KEEPING SECRETS   (1291, $3.75)
by Suzanne Morris
It was 1914, the winds of war were sweeping the globe, and Electra was in the eye of the hurricane—rushing headlong into a marriage with the wealthy Emory Cabot. Her days became a carousel of European dignitaries, rich investors, and worldly politicians. And her nights were filled with mystery and passion . . . .

Available wherever paperbacks are sold, or order direct from the Publisher. Send cover price plus 50¢ per copy for mailing and handling to Zebra Books, 475 Park Avenue South, New York, N.Y. 10016. DO NOT SEND CASH.

EXCITING BESTSELLERS FROM ZEBRA

STORM TIDE (1230, $3.75)
by Patricia Rae
In a time when it was unladylike to desire one man, defiant, flamehaired Elizabeth desired two! And while she longed to be held in the strong arms of a handsome sea captain, she yearned for the status and wealth that only the genteel doctor could provide—leaving her hopelessly torn amidst passion's raging STORM TIDE . . . .

PASSION'S REIGN (1177, $3.95)
by Karen Harper
Golden-haired Mary Bullen was wealthy, lovely and refined—and lusty King Henry VIII's prize gem! But her passion for the handsome Lord William Stafford put her at odds with the Royal Court. Mary and Stafford lived by a lovers' vow: one day they would be ruled by only the crown of PASSION'S REIGN.

HEIRLOOM (1200, $3.95)
by Eleanora Brownleigh
The surge of desire Thea felt for Charles was powerful enough to convince her that, even though they were strangers and their marriage was a fake, fate was playing a most subtle trick on them both: Were they on a mission for President Teddy Roosevelt—or on a crusade to realize their own passionate desire?

LOVESTONE (1202, $3.50)
by Deanna James
After just one night of torrid passion and tender need, the darkhaired, rugged lord could not deny that Moira, with her precious beaty, was born to be a princess. But how could he grant her freedom when he himself was a prisoner of her love?

Available wherever paperbacks are sold, or order direct from the Publisher. Send cover price plus 50¢ per copy for mailing and handling to Zebra Books, 475 Park Avenue South, New York, N.Y. 10016. DO NOT SEND CASH.